IN LANGUAGE AND IN LOVE

MARGUERITE DURAS: THE UNSPEAKABLE

𝖲𝖼𝗋𝗂𝗉𝗍𝖺 𝖧𝗎𝗆𝖺𝗇𝗂𝗌𝗍𝗂𝖼𝖺®

Directed by
BRUNO M. DAMIANI
The Catholic University of America

ADVISORY BOARD

IN LANGUAGE AND IN LOVE

MARGUERITE DURAS: THE UNSPEAKABLE

ESSAYS FOR MARGUERITE DURAS

Edited by

Mechthild Cranston

1992

𝕾cripta 𝕳umanistica

101

Library of Congress Cataloging-in-Publication Data

In language and in love Marguerite Duras : the unspeakable ; essays
  for Marguerite Duras / edited by Mechthild Cranston.
        p.   cm. -- (Scripta Humanistica ; 101)
    Includes bibliographical references.
    ISBN 0-916379-97-3 : $46.50
    1. Duras, Marguerite--Criticism and interpretation.   I. Cranston,
  Mechthild.   II. Series: Scripta Humanistica (Series) ; 101.
  PQ2607.U8245Z745   1992
  843'.912--dc20   92-16717
                                                                  CIP

Publisher and Distributor:
SCRIPTA HUMANISTICA
1383 Kersey Lane
Potomac, Maryland 20854 U.S.A.

For *M.D.*
& Mother

Je n'ai jamais rien fait qu'attendre devant la porte fermée.

Marguerite Duras: *L'Amant*

TABLE OF CONTENTS

INTRODUCTION

Mechthild Cranston

Even before the appearance of *L'Amant de la Chine du Nord* on the Paris scene last summer (come to dislodge, even before *its* release, Jean-Jacques Annaud's film version of Marguerite Duras' earlier *L'Amant*, Prix Goncourt 1984)[1] and prior to the debates sparked by the new *Lover* in publications like *Libération, Le Monde, Le Nouvel Observateur*, and *Le Point* (June 1991),[2] more than two dozen scholars on this side of the Atlantic suggested to the Modern Language Association of America meeting in San Francisco a session on "Marguerite Duras: The Unspeakable." From among the many interesting articles received, eight were chosen to make up the present anthology, meant not to displace, but to com-

---

[1] "Le film n'aura rien à voir avec *L'Amant de la Chine du Nord*, qui maintenant est pour moi le véritable *Amant*" (*Le Monde*, 13 juin 1991), said Marguerite Duras. After the film's opening in Paris, Danièle Heymann wrote, "Mais là où l'affaire devient belle, exemplaire même, c'est que ce conflit s'est révélé fécond. Prenant sa source dans *L'Amant*, le roman, séparant deux créateurs incompatibles, il a donné naissance à deux œuvres nouvelles et accomplies. Comme le fleuve Mékong écarte les bras en son delta, *L'Amant* est devenu un film de Jean-Jacques Annaud, *L'Amant* est devenu un autre livre de Marguerite Duras, *L'Amant de la Chine du Nord*" (*Le Monde*, 23 janvier 1992).

[2] Constructed around questions regarding "truth" and authorial reliability.

1

plement Sanford Ames' 1988 collection, *Remains to be Seen*, the first volume of essays in English devoted to Marguerite Duras.[3]

From the beginning, our title vacillated between the *unspeakable* and the *unnamable*, the word and the fiction, the person and the persona of Marguerite Duras. Opting, finally, for *Marguerite Duras: The Unspeakable*, we are, of course, aware of that title's inherent ambiguity and contradiction, since the essays presented here do indeed speak—and at length—of *Hiroshima mon amour*, 1960; *Le Ravissement de Lol V. Stein*, 1964; *Le Vice-consul*, 1965; *La Maladie de la mort*, 1982; *Emily L.*, 1987; *La Pluie d'été*, 1990; *L'Amant* and *L'Amant de la Chine du Nord*, raising, along the way, the larger issues of language and madness, "truth" and "translation,"[4] autobiography and fiction, restoration and deception,[5] the historical fact and the private myth of "celle qui n'est pas

---

3 Several of the primary works discussed here (*Emily L.*, *La Pluie d'été*, *L'Amant de la Chine du Nord*) and many of the critical studies referenced (Hewitt, Hofmann, Ricouart, Vircondelet) had, of course, not appeared at the time of Ames' anthology in which he states, "The career of Marguerite Duras as a writer almost exactly spans the years from the bomb dropped on Hiroshima to the exhibit called 'Les Immatériaux,' organized at the Beaubourg Museum of Paris, from March 28 to July 25, 1985, by Jean-François Lyotard [. . .] ," unaware, as yet, of that other bomb to be dropped some seven years later by "Dame Marguerite" herself in *L'Amant de la Chine du Nord*.

4 "[L']Amant n'est pas un récit autobiographique, c'est une traduction," said Marguerite Duras in the *Le Monde* interview of 13 June 1991. She has stated publicly both that the story of her life does not exist and that *L'Amant* is completely autobiographical.

5 "[L']œuvre durassienne se joue tout entière sur la ruine d'une biographie impossible, entre restauration et duperie," writes Jean-Louis Ezine in *Le Nouvel Observateur* (13-19 juin 1991).

nommée," the unnamed and perhaps unnamable child of *L'Amant*, the *in-fans* of the Durassian universe that turns on the Pacific and Hiroshima, on Auschwitz and Never(s).

"Books," John Knowles declared during a recent reading from his autobiography, "books come out of trees." For us, the listeners, Knowles' unfinished autobiography also came, of course, out of the mouth of the speaker. Against[6] the biographical/biological testing ground of the *authorial*, the essays collected here seek the *textual* body, a visual plane which, probed deeply, may surrender a voice, if not yet a name.[7]

Speaking of Balzac's novels, Duras has said, "His books are indigestible. There's no place for the reader," which, fortunately, does not keep her from adding, in the same interview, "Balzac was my earliest nourishment."[8] Reflecting on the contemporary cinema, Duras commented, "Il faut de l'air. On ne re-

---

6 That is, attempting the contradiction of at once leaning against and opposing.

7 "L'écriture reste première. Encore que *La Pluie d'été* a été provoqué par le film *les Enfants*. Maintenant, j'ai envie de faire un nouveau film à partir du livre. Je vais de moi à moi. C'est ça, le narcissisme," commented Duras to *Le Monde*. "Avant *les Enfants*, il y avait déjà un texte," asks the interviewer. "Qui s'appelait *Ah Ernesto!*" replies Duras.

8 *New York Sunday Times Literary Supplement*, 20 October 1991. Would she also deny today, we wonder, her early passion for—and inspiration drawn from—Victor Hugo, recently reported by Danièle Heymann in *Le Monde* (23 janvier 1992) and Alain Vircondelet in his latest *Duras*?

spire plus dans les films [. . .] moi, j'ai ça."[9] The "open" air, the breath for which she herself must now struggle, physically,[10] is the in-spiration Duras offers her listener, the place she makes for the reader in the silences and empty spaces of her texts. Into the blanks thus created, the contributors to this anthology—come from different national and critical backgrounds, and at various stages of their careers—have placed their divergent views and interpretations of the Durassian œuvre.

In the opening essay, "Dame Duras: Breaking Through the Text," Thomas Spear introduces the problem of referential readings and the person/persona inquiry: Duras the media event, and Duras the "fictional" exponent of, among other things, homosexuality, rape, and incest. Spears shows how the more "acceptable" social taboos (like madness, adultery, alcoholism and murder) of the early works (e.g., *Moderato cantabile*, 1958; *Dix heures et demie du soir en été* and *Hiroshima mon amour*, 1960; *Le Ravissement de Lol V. Stein*, 1964) are superseded, beginning in the 1980s, by the more unspeakable transgressions of *La Pute de la côte normande* and *Les Yeux bleus cheveux noirs*, 1986, the latter dedicated to Yann Andréa, Duras' young homosexual companion since *L'Eté 80*.[11] Against the paratext—and, more particularly, the epitext (staying in the Genettian

---

[9] "Elle montre l'appareil qui lui troue la gorge," adds the interviewer for *Le Monde.*

[10] Following her tracheotomy of 1990.

[11] Who made their relationship public in *M.D.*, the harrowing account of Marguerite Duras' detoxification cure at the American hospital in 1982.

idiom)—of television, radio and journalistic interviews, Spear tests Duras' film, theater, and "autofiction" (a term he borrows from Serge Doubrovsky), showing how, in the end, an author of best-sellers and an icon of popular culture[12] subject to parody and pastiche, Duras "willingly exhibits her persona" to the reader turned voyeur who breaks through the fictional framework of her text.[13]

Rachael Criso's "*Elle est une Autre.* The Duplicity of Self in *L'Amant*" also conducts an inquiry into the Durassian person/persona, but her essay is text-specific and starts from a different critical stance. Recalling Leo Spitzer's distinction between the "poetic I" and the "empirical I," Criso examines the *je/elle* dichotomy in *L'Amant.* She demonstrates (convincingly, I think) that, contrary to common expectation and historical precedent, Duras reserves first-person narration to the telling of public events, while using the third-person pronoun to deal with experiences of the private self. Criso discusses Duras' family relationships which may have influenced the splitting narrative voice, and the "unspeakable" subject matter of her adult life. The fact that the *je* and *elle* of *L'Amant* were fused into the third-person *enfant* of *L'Amant de la Chine du Nord*, should invite

---

[12] Consecrated in titles like the *Globe*'s "Duras est sexy." A recent interview (*Le Monde*, 23 janvier 1992) reminds us that *L'Amant* has sold over two million copies to date and has been translated into 43 languages. A *succès de scandale*, or a true appreciation of Duras' unique contribution to contemporary fiction?

[13] Which may, in the end, enslave Duras in her own image. "Plus Marguerite est libre de l'histoire vécue," writes the commentator of *Le Nouvel Observateur*, "plus elle est prisonnière de la légende inventée."

5

further investigation into the choices of fictional telling.

Focusing, again, on a single work, Julia Lauer-Chéenne's essay titled, "The Unspeakable Heroine of *Emily L.*," likewise questions the transgressions of *je* and *elle*. She explores the "gap between representation and experience" into which writing slips as a process of discovery aided by nonverbal communication like the gazing or *nonregard* of an Other that produces both "erasure and projection" in indistinct landscapes of stories told and silenced. With the look of the *nonregard*, Lauer-Chéenne contrasts the gaze "that projects, doubles, and fascinates" in its search for the originary (unnamed) suffering that lies at the core of the text like the destroyed poem come to signify the doubly-displaced prose tale (as well as the impossible love of Emily L). In the tension between the spoken and the *interdit*, Duras writes, to borrow a Kristevan term, her *sujet-en-procès*, the *inter-dit* of the unspeakable.

A reading informed by Kristeva and Cixous is offered by Marie-France Etienne in "Loss, Abandonment, and Love: The Ego in Exile," which enters *La Pluie d'été* via the "livre brûlé" whose absent center may be found, she argues, in the woman's body, come to voice in the mother's wordless Russian lullaby, "La Neva."[14] The mother is at the heart of *La Pluie d'été* (and, indeed, at the heart of the whole Durassian œuvre), "the chora" ($\chi\omega\rho\alpha$) in or around which the children (and Duras' readers) must do their daring

---

[14] Which recalls to this reader, at least phonically, the Nevers of *Hiroshima*.

dance: mother-lover-child-lover, love-death-love.[15] Only in his relationship to the (m)other's body does Emilio, the father (a foreigner), acquire his *droit de cité* in the body of the text. Abandoned by the mother, the children live in the *appentis*, leaning toward, but separate from the house, *apprentices* in the space of the unnamable where, ironically, names are found. In Etienne's view, the *appentis* becomes "a creative womb which subverts the symbolic." Here Ernesto, the eldest son, enters the (w)hole of the book that "tells the name of Oedipus and the silence of Jocasta," and, finally, his own story.[16] Here he recovers the "mot" which Lacan qualified as "ce qui se tait," language which expresses "the anarchic impulses and energies of the semiotic" in a space of reconciliation between Mother and Father, self and Other, silence and speech.

Another song without words, "*Battambang*: The Unnamable," is heard against the background of the Kristevan chora in Robin Lydenberg's discussion of *Le Ravissement de Lol V. Stein* and *Le Vice-consul*. Like "La Neva," "Battambang" has the force of the uncanny. At once familiar and foreign, it is a sort of talisman that "both attracts and repels." Wordless and diffuse, it can be re-membered only in the rhythm of footsteps matched to a faltering speech which in the very act of naming mocks the power of the signifier to designate and mean. The anonymous beggarwoman who aimlessly wanders about singing of Battambang

---

15 "J'adore la mère dans *La Pluie d'été* [. . .]," says Duras. "C'est ma vie, la mère" (*Le Monde,* 13 juin 1991).

16 And ours. "Ernesto c'est toute l'humanité," said Duras to the interviewer from *Le Monde*.

speaks nothing but "des discours inutiles dans le silence profond." And yet "Battambang" may point to something beyond the limits of language: in the patterns of the dance, in the semiotic gestures of eye and hand, in the cries (of laughter and of pain) which, Lydenberg suggests, men and women may approach—and hear—differently.

Julia Balén's "Duras' 'Laughing Cure' for Lacan's Hysterical Lack" supports such a distinction in her discussion of *La Maladie de la mort*. A tale of desire that plays upon the structures of both romance and pornography, Duras' *Maladie*—by suppressing names and clearly gendered participants in the Freudian *fort-da* game—subverts the objectifying (male) gaze of Lacanian readings (and of the genres it parodies). Addressed to an unnamed male listener and to a self-reflective narrator (à la Butor) whom we are meant to see as male (even though the text does not state a gender), Duras' "you" also calls to the reader who will have to make his/her own gendered choices. This triple subject "you" (narrator/listener/you), Balén argues, subverts the masculinized gaze, the dominant view of white Western culture scrutinized by Duras. Twice in the work, control is further eroded by the emergence of a first-person narrator who gazes upon "you," whose thoughts and feelings "I" claims not to know at the very moment of "your" *jouissance*. *She,* the traditional *object* of desire, becomes the *subject* of *your* tears, clouding your vision, exposing your malady. To your (and Lacan's) hysterical weeping, Duras opposes *her* laughter: "Duras laughs in love."

Moving from the unspeakable to the unrepresentable, the essay by Anne-Marie Gronhovd and William VanderWolk, "Memory as Ontological Disruption: *Hiroshima mon amour* as a Postmodern

Work," stands near the end of our anthology: a *memento mori* and a (false) coda. False, because the authors view *Hiroshima* as an open-ended work of infinite regression and referral.[17] Informed by Ihab Hassan and Jean-François Lyotard[18] they examine how through fragmentation, indeterminacy, subversion, polychronicity, silence and repetition, *Hiroshima mon amour* eludes epistemological inquiry and logical (re)construction. At the heart of the matter (screenplay and film) memory functions no longer as a tool for recovery, but as an agent of disjunction and subversion. No longer "à la recherche du temps perdu" that celebrates, at its conclusion, "le temps retrouvé," Duras sets her story into a spatialized time—at once Hiroshima and Never(s)—around which fragmented images and repetitive sounds (music and dialogue) perform their "postmodern dance of indeterminate content and form." Language displaces the visual ("l'écriture reste première," Duras will later say) because the screen memory ultimately sought by *Hiroshima* is unrepresentable. "She" saw it only in a film; "He" wasn't there; "they" that were, are dead or blind. In the end, as the personal *histoire* of "Elle" and "Lui" passes into the global *Histoire* of history, language itself erases the fragile borders of "reality," plunging us into the silence of postmodernity, or into the unspeakable of madness: "Tu n'as *rien* vu à Hiroshima. Rien."

Madness which, in our final offering, Inger Gilbert traces back to the beginnings of Western thought in

---

[17] And all Durassian readings and writings are without closure.

[18] Whose Paris exhibit of "Les Immatériaux" marked, according to Sanford Ames, the end of Duras' career as a writer (cf. note 3 above).

her essay, "Imagination into Myth: Love (Language) as Madness in Plato and Duras." Assuming that, like Beckett's, Duras' is a world of "Imagination dead," Gilbert shows how the Beckettian imperative to "imagine" nevertheless floods that world with an outpouring of "love" not sanctioned by Christian, Romantic, or Freudian tradition. Seeking its roots in Plato's *Phaedrus*, Gilbert defines Duras' love as divinely inspired madness, "fraught with the highest bliss."

"Fraught" because for Duras as for Plato, says Gilbert, love, like language, is both "the measure and the prison-house of human identity." We *fall* in love because we remember an always already lost and perfect original beyond. Their wings clipped, Duras' lovers have nothing but language and image to (at)tempt transcendence: *Hiroshima mon amour.*[19] Language itself, however absurd, thus becomes illumination from within, its own protagonist that falters, according to Gilbert, not because of a lack (Lacanian or otherwise), but because of a fullness of meaning beyond words. Writing, then, becomes the touchstone (but also the tombstone) of the unnamable other "authenticated" in death: the *translatio* of an always already prior but ultimately irretrievable text. "Lost beyond living and telling,"[20] Dachau and *La Douleur*,

---

[19] One day, Marguerite Duras recalls, three Japanese men came to her door asking her to remake *Hiroshima* in Japan. "Vous avez Platon, Shakespeare, Racine. Nous, nous avons Hiroshima," they said (*Libération*, 13 juin 1991).

[20] To adapt the beautiful title of Richard Stamelman's most recent book on modern French poetry. All texts referenced in these essays are identified in the "Selective Bibliography" given at the end of the volume.

the *seduction* of a name: "Marguerite Duras: The Unspeakable." In language and in love. In love and madness.[21]

*

Many have helped to see these essays into print. I thank my collaborators for having undertaken—with patience and good cheer—numerous revisions of their manuscripts; I am grateful to Philip Cranston for his diligent proofreading; to Sandi Piazza for her mainframe wizardry, and to *M.D.* for having brought together these happy few: readers/writers willing to listen and wait *devant la porte fermée.*

[21] "Indicible, hélas, serait alors le mot pour cette séduction," concludes Jean-Louis Ezine in *Le Nouvel Observateur.*

I

DAME DURAS:
BREAKING THROUGH THE TEXT

Thomas Spear

Marguerite Duras has become a fictional persona, a questionably autobiographical character placed on public exhibition. The author's personal creation and obsession is Marguerite Duras. With a stream of autobiographical writing and through numerous interviews, Duras' fictional focus has undeniably shifted to herself. As Aliette Armel writes, it was in the film *Le Camion* that Duras, "la Dame au camion," first discovered "la liberté de la parole autobiographique et médiatique" (89) by acting the principal role created for herself. Duras has developed an art of framing, especially in film, even when the public's attention is drawn to silence or nothingness. Now that her creative attention has become self-centered, she has stepped into the narrative terrain established in the context of her fictional world, becoming and surpassing a composite of her women protagonists.

Through various forms of prose narrative, theater, and film, Duras develops a portrait of her life and career as a politically engaged writer and film maker. In the process, the identity of the fictional Duras becomes entangled with her public persona. Her alcohol abuse, for example, can become a joke (*Les Parleuses*

218) or a serious problem (*La Vie matérielle* 20-25), part of her fictional and real worlds. In self-parody, Duras dresses her real-life characters in a "look Duras" (*La Vie matérielle* 75). Her mediated interviews encourage a continuity with that established by her narrative framework; she wills her public to accept this composite life story, a *fait divers* of rape and incest, alcohol and passion. She tells Bernard Pivot, "Vous avez beau fouiller, j'ai vraiment vécu comme tout le monde." Nonetheless, she invites her reader, spectator, and listener to pry into the details of her life, to delve with her into the narrative of her childhood, and to believe in her fiction.

The Durassian identity is forced upon her readers, like a stage character who might reveal to her audience that she is not an actress but a woman speaking of her own life. Duras' commercial success has become such that, on the eve of the release of *L'Amant de la Chine du Nord* on June 14, 1991, she could arrange double-page promotional interviews in both *Le Monde* and *Libération* and, a week later, appear on the nationally broadcast "Caractères" television program hosted by Bernard Rapp. Naming off most every item of the text as true (including herself: "Moi, c'est vrai"), she told the journalist from *Libération* that she returned to the novel because it is "libre, désintéressé." The novel form does indeed free her from an audience's expectation to tell the truth, but her novels are not "dis-interested." They are carefully constructed to coincide with her extratextual maneuvering of her readers' response. By securing her text's presence in the media, she locks this paratextual interpretation into the reading of her works.

Duras makes use of public communication channels to affect interpretation, creating combinations of

13

fictive and autobiographical forms. In her first novels, the author's identity is never directly linked with her protagonists; in the last works, an unnamed "she" is extratextually identified as Duras herself. She not only shifts her identity into that of a fictive character, but becomes this character in interviews. The multiple re-writing of the Durassian persona continually changes, from novel to interview and back into "fiction." Her life story has become theater: "On joue [ses] interviews maintenant" (*Le Nouvel Observateur*, 14-20 novembre 1986). The "Marguerite Duras" identity is established in her fictions as well as in public appearances: life and text play with and against one another. Duras breaks out of a purely textual mold and becomes the "Duras" persona.

Like her character Suzanne before a movie screen in *Un Barrage contre le Pacifique*, Duras often leads her reader/spectator into a theatrical setting of imagined love or dreams, a fictional décor which is established before being reduced to nothingness by its categorical unreality. Suzanne (the role Duras bases on her own memories) enjoys escaping through dreams, as in a movie theater where she can be diverted from her goal of finding her brother. One afternoon, Suzanne enters this cinematic space of symbiotic empathy and becomes engulfed in the romantic tale being shown:

> Le piano commença à jouer. La lumière s'éteignit. Suzanne se sentit désormais invisible, invincible et se mit à pleurer de bonheur. C'était l'oasis, la salle noire de l'après-midi, la nuit des solitaires, la nuit artificielle et démocratique, la grande nuit égalitaire du cinéma, plus vraie que la vraie nuit, plus ravissante, plus consolante que toutes les vraies nuits [. . .]. (188)

More real than reality itself, Suzanne's world of the movie theater resembles that of Duras' fiction. Suzanne's film is the love story of a beautiful young woman who has a number of unsuccessful adventures before finding love in Venice:

> [Ils] s'enlacent. Il dit je vous aime. Elle dit je vous aime aussi. Le ciel sombre de l'attente s'éclaire d'un coup. Foudre d'un tel baiser. Gigantesque communion de la salle de l'écran. On voudrait bien être à leur place. Ah! comme on le voudrait. (189)

The sheer plasticity in this display of sentiment is made obvious with the attention drawn to the performance space of the film projection. The feelings described maintain a quality of authenticity, nonetheless; their pure representation is immediately and universally understood (by the public in the movie theater, for example). Like the wall Suzanne's mother will have built to hold back the Pacific, the movie screen divides the real world of the spectator from the potential and imaginary world of the film with which Suzanne has "communion." Duras dramatically establishes such barriers in both content and form before breaking down their assault upon difference. Thus she will both acknowledge and attack the wall she builds between human beings and that which distinguishes her real life from its textual signifiers.

One can speak of a "wall" in Duras' works, even if such a wall is apparently both impossible and immaterial. Like a movie screen, it serves as a metaphor to discuss her method of reducing the separation between her public and the performative narration. This symbolic barrier would also separate Duras from her narrative autoportrait, and fiction from reality. In *Un Barrage contre le Pacifique*, Duras' wall becomes physically tangible, a dream rendered real by the dike built by French colonialists and indigenous village people. Constructed out of mangrove logs before being eaten by crabs and washed away by the sea, it is destroyed like a tumbled house of cards. No matter how futile it may seem to erect such a barrier, the sea wall is an attempt by the novel's protagonists to alter their torpid lives. The project to build it is destined to fail at conception as well as throughout its planned execution. The sea wall ends up as nothing but a big wet dream.

> Les barrages de la mère dans la plaine, c'était le grand malheur et la grande rigolade à la fois, ça dépendait des jours. C'était terrible et c'était marrant. Ça dépendait de quel côté on se plaçait, du côté de la mer qui les avait fichus en l'air, [. . .] ou au contraire, du côté de ceux qui avaient mis six mois à les construire dans l'oubli total des méfaits pourtant certains de la mer et des crabes. (53)

Like this wall which cannot hold back the Pacific, Duras' land of inventive fantasy is washed away by the sea of reality, not destroyed by it, but rather encompassed by the larger totality. Her fictive narrations, however solid or ravishing, are mere constructions of human dreams which melt into nothingness, elusively holding back the painful reality of human existence.

Duras loves placing her audience up against such walls. As in Suzanne's film, she frequently makes the framework of her narrative world visible through *mises-en-abyme* before breaking through the limiting boundaries of the artistic medium itself. The narration of *Les Yeux bleus cheveux noirs* is accompanied by a secondary text containing stage directions for the principal story. This is an example of Duras'

16

"couloirs scéniques," the "longs passages détachés du texte par une légère mise en retrait, mais intégrés pourtant à la compréhension de l'ensemble" (Armel 117). Using such typographical signposts, Duras makes the narrative framework visible. In *Les yeux bleus cheveux noirs*, she creates actors in this subtext who tell (in the conditional mode) how the principal text would be staged, a *mise-en-abyme* of the central plot through a theatrical reading of the characters' roles. The actors of this secondary text go to the edge of their textual possibility, approaching the point at which they would burst through the narrative walls of their respective characters:

> Si elle parlait, dit l'acteur, elle dirait: Si notre histoire se jouait au théâtre, un acteur irait au bord de la scène, au bord de la rivière de lumière, très près de vous et de moi, il serait habillé de blanc, il serait dans une concentration très grande de son attention, intéressé par lui-même au plus haut degré, tendu vers la salle comme vers lui-même. Il se présenterait comme l'homme de l'histoire, l'homme, dirait-on, dans son absence centrale, son irréversible extériorité. Il regarderait, comme vous avez tendance à le faire, vers l'extérieur des murs, comme si c'était possible, dans la direction de la trahison. (116-17)

Like the place of her own narrative and auto-biographical persona, the space for Duras' protagonists is specifically defined but constrictive; they want to enter into another realm, to jump through their narrative frame (cf. Willis 139). In the passage cited above, the characters' story is performed on a stage: the male actor is deeply concentrated on himself as well as on his public, but the space of his communication can be "betrayed" through a revelation of its framework, its very walls of fictitiousness. *Les Yeux bleus cheveux noirs* is complicated by multiple layers of acting and reality; an odor, for example, rises up in the subtextual theater and becomes "celle qui est écrite ici" (21), carrying its presence into the principal story. At the end, the external frame of the subtextual reading, previously described simply as a room of a theater, becomes that of a theater built with its backstage wall against the sea. The symbolic wall "betraying" the separation between fiction and reality is revealed, making the space of fiction real. The proposed theatrical reading places the actors against the background sea like the characters of the principal story. By staging the text in the subtext, its own reality is subsumed by its "realistic" theatrical (re)presentation.

Mise-en-abyme is but one form of metanarrative focus Duras uses to expose her narrative framework. Told in the *conditionnel parfait*, *Le Camion* begins with a metanarrative "it would have been a film, therefore it is a film." The "you" of *L'Homme atlantique* steps off-camera, even where, in the prose version of the film, there is no camera. As demonstrated with her "couloirs scéniques," Duras shows how a stage direction in a text draws attention to the textual form, its framework and its limitations. She also uses camera angles to allude to extratextual performances of the text in a modified form: plots and scenes recur in any of the distinct or composite ("texte/théâtre/film") narrative forms that Duras tends to "fusionner" (Armel 117). In *L'Amant de la Chine du Nord*, metanarrative focus serves to compare the novel to previous Durassian fictions. Often referring to "the book(s)" or "the other book(s)," this mirroring of previous works exposes the unnamed Marguerite Duras. The new version of *L'Amant* is strictly third-person narrative; the "she" and "I" of

L'Amant have been fused into "she," who speaks of "le premier livre," what was said elsewhere: "Et encore elle le dit ici" (78-79). The intertextual borrowing, or "self-plagiarism" to which she readily admits (e.g., "Apostrophes" and *L'Amant de la Chine du Nord*), puts metanarrative focus on "this book" when it is compared to the extratextual works to which Duras refers, either through reference within the text (e.g., 52) or by listing, in footnotes, the titles of her earlier novels and films.

Duras' narrators can openly declare that they are prone to invention or lying (cf. Armel 148ff); the visible narrative framework in which they exist is equally invented and untrustworthy. Duras forces her public to confront the existing (but artificial, theatrical) "barriers" which frame her narrations, before expounding upon the futility of any attempt to transcend this visible framework and to achieve communication. The autobiographical enterprise of her late career carries with it a barrier of incommunicability, since the non-fictive identity is structured by means of the multiple (and often unreliable) framework of text and interview, film and theatrical performance.

Serge Doubrovsky's term "autofiction" may serve to describe Duras' dubiously autobiographical, self-conscious terrain. He defines "autofiction" as that

> fausse fiction, qui est l'histoire d'une vraie vie, le texte, de par le mouvement de son écriture, se déloge instantanément du registre patenté du réél. Ni autobiographie ni roman, donc, au sens strict, il fonctionne dans l'entre-deux, en un renvoi incessant, en un lieu impossible et insaisissable que dans l'opération du texte. (69-70)

Aliette Armel has studied the development of the autobiographical revelations in Duras, who is directly involved in this autofictional act, "abolissant la distance que la littérature établit entre la vie et l'œuvre" (109). According to Armel, Duras writes from the position of "absence," an absence or distancing from one's self in order to

> mettre le réel à distance, considérer l'expérience comme un objet d'étude extérieur à soi et intimement lié à des éléments issus de l'imaginaire. L'importance du vécu est capitale, masse écrasante, source inépuisable de fascination dont l'écrit opère une perpétuelle recréation en y introduisant, fatalement, des aspects venus du monde du rêve [. . .]. (Armel 137)

Ultimately giving priority to the text rather than to the life represented, Duras writes autofiction, having "confié le langage d'une aventure à l'aventure du langage" (Doubrovsky 69). The autobiographical identity is defined and, of course, fictionalized in the language of the text. Duras' life has become the primary sustenance of her fiction, especially in her late works which Armel calls the "Yann Andréa cycle."

In an autofiction such as those of Doubrovsky, multiple games are played on the names of the author/narrator. In works prior to the 1980s, Duras transformed her life into fictive narrative (and/or film and theater) where the protagonists often had names other than the simple "she" or "I" the author now uses and identifies with herself. The autobiographical identity is never specifically made with the name "Marguerite Duras." Rare occurrences of the initials "M.D." or the name "Duras" appear, but more frequently in texts which can be called interviews (like *La Vie matérielle* and *Les Parleuses*) than in novels.

Whereas in *L'Amant* Duras uses both the first- and third-person pronouns for the narrated past and the narrating present of her narrator/character, her pivot of autobiographical identity in *L'Amant de la Chine du Nord* is the third-person pronoun "elle," maintained throughout the narration to describe both "the child" of the story and "elle" who remembers the past of this child:

> Elle se souvient. Elle est la dernière à se souvenir encore. Elle entend encore le bruit de la mer dans la chambre. D'avoir écrit ça, elle se souvient aussi, comme le bruit de la rue chinoise. (78)

Duras' visible efforts to avoid naming her "fictional" characters could prevent their inclusion among works of autobiography in which, as Philippe Lejeune defines it, the author identifies him- or herself *within* the work as the narrator-character, a link made to the name and identity of the author on the book's cover (26). In *L'Amant de la Chine du Nord*, Duras in essence makes this link of identity within the text yet without using her proper name. The textual "she" of this novel is nameless: "Elle, c'est celle qui n'a de nom dans le premier livre ni dans celui qui l'avait précédé ni dans celui-ci" (13). The third-person "she" nonetheless incarnates the identity which mirrors back to the author. As mentioned, previous works by Duras are precisely named in footnotes, and Duras explicitly identifies with this narrative persona in frequent and unambiguous extratextual declarations. As paratext (especially in television and press interviews), these declarations become an implicit part of the reading (of the textual reality). Since, however, these interviews reveal the storyteller's love to enchant listeners with em-bellished modifications, we can see how they con-tribute to the autofictive creation of the Marguerite Duras character.

As Armel argues, Duras' writing turns toward the autobiographical around 1980. An analysis of the Marguerite Duras character as presented in the press shows that the author also sympathizes with previous protagonists, like Lol V. Stein, Anne-Marie Stretter, and Suzanne of *Un Barrage contre le Pacifique*, as well as with the post-1980 "I" and/or "she" of *L'Amant*, *Les Yeux bleus cheveux noirs*, *Emily L.* and *L'Amant de la Chine du Nord*. She has made it impossible to distinguish life from text in her recent, most candidly autobiographical works which Armel justifiably finds to be a "fusion totale entre le texte et l'existence de celui qui écrit" (159). A portrait of Duras based on interviews compares reasonably well with that of her fictional characters, which complicates a reader's efforts to distinguish biographical detail from invention.

Subjects which the Occident censors (such as vi-olent and/or passionate sex, alcoholism, and incest) are frequently and audaciously displayed in Duras' works. The woman's body in *La Maladie de la mort* which beckons to be strangled and raped (21) exemplifies how Duras solicits passionate reactions to her stories of love-making. Many of her women lovers carry with them an aura of prostitution which she will also attribute to herself. Near the end of *L'Amant de la Chine du Nord*, Duras hints that the young girl was regularly raped: "ce viol chaque nuit du corps maigre" (212). Up to this point, however, the "child" was more than a willing participant in the lovemaking (according to Duras, "si la femme jouit, il n'y a plus de viol" [*Les Parleuses* 44]). Through sensationalist variation, Duras invites a re-evaluation of her character.

She makes public autobiographical revelations in the discussion of her alcoholism. Duras and Yann Andréa have both published books which tell of the period of her detoxification at the American Hospital in Neuilly (home to such other drawn-out and painful internments as that of Simone de Beauvoir's mother in *Une mort très douce*). In *M.D.*—which happens to be the American abbreviation for medical doctors—Andréa gives his account of Duras' period of alcohol "rehabilitation." In *La Vie matérielle*, she tells her version of her bouts with alcohol and evokes her withdrawal hallucinations.

The 1990s reader can thus draw parallels with some of her "fictional" characters. In Peter Brook's interpretation of *Moderato cantabile* (a film Duras hates), Jeanne Moreau beautifully renders the alcoholic impulses of Duras' Anne Desbaresdes. One would have to search much further than Hemingway to find any work of fiction where the characters drink as heavily as those in Duras' *Le Marin de Gibraltar*. Within the novel, functioning as a *mise-en-abyme*, there is an "American" novel ("A cause des whiskys. Le whisky est un alcool américain" [204]) which the male narrator would write about Anna, "l'ivrognissime des mers du Sud" (376), who roams the world on her yacht. This marathon drinking adventure, supplemented with other prominent episodes of booze-guzzling in Duras' writing (such as that of Maria in *Dix heures et demie du soir en été*, who drinks her manzanillas in a very Hemingway-American style), adds up to more than a simple characterizing device. The temptation to draw a connection between Duras' fictional world and the author's own alcoholism is great. If we are to believe what she writes in the section entitled "L'alcool" of *La Vie matérielle*, Duras began drinking when she was forty-one. Through modifications of her self-characterization, however, she prevents any single interpretation of her fiction based on biographical association. In *L'Amant de la Chine du Nord*, "she" began drinking (alcoholic *choum* with her Chinese lover) at age fifteen . . .

Such efforts to compare the author's life with her fiction lead to biographical criticism worthy of Sainte-Beuve: everything against which artists have long fought. An author's life is distinct from the created work.   Yet, as Gérard Genette has shown, a text is always "accompanied" by a paratext. The paratext includes, in addition to the "peritext" (prefaces, titles, marginal notes, etc.), the "epitext": external "accessories" such as interviews and correspondence.   And, Genette believes, the paratext is determined by the author's intention and responsibility (*Palimpsestes* 9; *Seuils* 7-10). Duras makes use of her wide access to the media to firmly and willfully establish this paratextual identity which exposes the autobiographical elements of her fictions.

As Sharon Willis writes, Duras crosses "the boundary between 'difficult' and popular fiction" (8). With *L'Amant*, she emerged from the relatively restricted circle of admirers and fans ("ceux qui m'aimaient depuis longtemps," *Le Nouvel Observateur*, 14-20 novembre 1986) to become a media event.   Once established, her popularity makes good press. "Duras est sexy!" titles *Globe* magazine (juillet-août 1988), knowing that many issues can be sold with Duras' name on the cover and a story she tells of a man jerking off against her at a very important reception. John Waters included an homage to Dame Marguerite in *Polyester* (1981), his first film aimed at a commercial audience. At his drive-in movie theater, which impresses Francine Fishpaw (Divine) as being "high brow," the marquee is lit with:

> 3 MARGUERITE DURAS NITE
> THE TRUCK INDIA SONG
> DESTROY SHE SAID

This very brief homage which has flashed across American movie screens is itself an ironic reflection of Duras' previous obscurity among the uninitiated suburbanites of middle America whom Waters ridicules and who would hardly break down the gates to sit through the triple feature of the marginally appealing films advertised. Duras does not aim for popular audiences in her own films, where the speed is slower than slow: "Il n'y a aucune urgence, jamais, ici" (*Les Parleuses* 126); hers are not common, action-packed, Hollywood adventures. Nor is she concerned with reassuring realism: "Le ton réaliste des films, je ne peux plus le supporter" (ibid. 134). Before the release of *L'Amant*, the Duras personality was shared among a select group of admirers who rarely brought her out of her relative obscurity.

As Duras has become a massively best-selling author, the creation of her character has been slipping out of her personal control. An amusing example of this can be found in the satire of Duras and pastiche of her style in *Virginie Q.* by "Marguerite Duraille," a novel "presented" by Patrick Rambaud. Whereas John Waters' homage is comically respectful, Rambaud's pastiche shows how the Durassian character can become ridiculously stereotyped. Rambaud's facetious title (which cannot translate into English) mocks that of *Emily L.* This lampoon is composed of clever repetitions of words dear to Duras—*ça, peut-être, souvent, rien, forcément*—and ridicules such Durassian themes as "la douleur" and endless crying (seen in many works but anticipating particularly well the copious spouts of tears in *L'Amant de la Chine du Nord*). Rambaud successfully reduces the 1980s popularity of Duras to a joke, using her imitable style which includes, as she has qualified it, "un report à la fin du mot majeur. Du mot qui compte" (*Le Nouvel Observateur*, 24-30 mai 1990). He parodies her talents as writer in a minimalist scenario of "Romeo and Juliette," through a Durassian *fait divers*, in an interview with a boxer named Ramirez, and in a story centered on garbage collectors and people drinking. Duras describes her syntax in terms which invite pastiche. Her infamous "écriture courante" can often sound more like a wheezing horse; as she says, "Je la laisse dans un état pantelant, la phrase" (*M.D. à Montréal* 64). Her prose invites cheap imitations of its self-conscious preciosity: "Ça, et, en plus, envie de manger David à chaque fois et des pleurs et, etc." ([sic] *L'Eté 80* 58); "C'est ça, ça va. Ça n'avance pas. Ça va nulle part, ça bouge" (*Les Parleuses* 16). Duras calls the dialogues toward the end of *L'Amant de la Chine du Nord* "chaotiques" (203, the quotation marks are her own); but the examples given are curiously less "chaotic" than those found in her usual, fragmentary style. Rambaud's pastiche shows how Duras has become a popular icon. Imitations and reproductions of her style help shape an extra-textual identity for which she is no longer entirely responsible.

Textual autobiographical identity can be presented by means of photographs, as used, for example, in Roland Barthes' fragmentary *Roland Barthes*. First titled *L'Image absolue*, *L'Amant* was written to accompany a series of photographs Duras' son had assembled. According to Alain Robbe-Grillet, the commissioned text and photographs were refused by the original editor because the text was too long. So when it appeared without the photographs, a certain element of the autobiographical connection was lost. *Les Lieux de Marguerite Duras*, published several years earlier, is Duras' best autobiographical effort to link her fictions and films, through photographs, with her personal life. Speaking of the missing central photograph in *L'Amant* (which would depict the young girl's meeting of the Chinese man on the Mekong river ferry), Leah Hewitt writes that "the status of the imaginary photo insists on autobiography's creative construction of the self-image, without, however, completely undermining the reference to a lived past" (112). In filmed television interviews of herself and in *Le Camion*, Duras presents an alternative photographic self-portrait but maintains this "creative" or fictional image of her published still photographs. She tells Jérôme Beaujour: "Il y a donc deux petites filles et moi dans ma vie. Celle du *Barrage*. Celle de *L'Amant*. Et celle des pho-

tographies de famille" (*La Vie matérielle* 88-89).
Any one of these little Marguerites is, and is not,
the real Duras. Photographic images of the past,
whether missing in the fiction (*L'Amant*) or present
in an interview (*Les Lieux de Marguerite Duras*),
confirm the difficulty of faithful re-creation of the
autobiographical identity.

Short, sensationalist news items, or *faits divers*,
often form the basis of Duras' stories, as in
*L'Amante anglaise, Dix heures et demie du soir en
été, La Pluie d'été*, and some of *La Vie matérielle*.
In the press, Duras frequently demonstrates this
fascination with the passions and crimes of ordinary and unknown people. It comes as no surprise,
therefore, that she would foster the cult of her own
personality as a character of a *fait divers*. She gives
supplements to the "Duras story" every time she
grants interviews to newspaper, magazine, and
television journalists. Her easy access to a huge
public has enabled her to interweave the incidents
of her documented public life with an intricate
fabric of fiction. This life is a *fait divers* in performance, starring Marguerite Duras in the leading
role, as in *Le Camion* or on television. She knows
how to manipulate her public's reception of her
character. Like the voyeur in the love triangle so
often represented in her fiction, the public becomes
her intermediary needed to communicate with her
portrait. Mirroring and unmasking acts include
their opposites: her identity is colored by her own
distorting interventions and by the interviewer's
leading questions, as seen in *Les Parleuses*. The
mystification which results continues to generate a
reading of Duras' fiction as reality, and her reality
as fiction. The self-portrait she re-creates in every

text and modifies in every interview consistently encourages her readers not to do otherwise but to merge the various forms of the Duras character into one identity.

Duras' feminist identity includes a particularly curious attitude toward men. She claims to hate them and thus speaks of her "insupportabilité des mecs" (*Le Nouvel Observateur*, 24-30 mai 1990). She also speaks of the need to love men to overcome this hate:

> Il faut beaucoup aimer les hommes. Beaucoup, beaucoup. Beaucoup les aimer pour les aimer. Sans cela, ce n'est pas possible, on ne peut pas les supporter.
> (*La Vie matérielle* 47)

It was a man, Jacques Lacan, she says, who rehabilitated *Lol V. Stein* (*Les Parleuses* 161) and another, Raymond Queneau, who promoted *Un Barrage contre le Pacifique* because he was "crazy" about it (*Le Nouvel Observateur*, 14-20 novembre 1986). She is as outspoken in her appreciation of these men as she is in reprobation of those like Philippe Sollers. She reverses the macho male gaze upon women; in *Le Marin de Gibraltar*, for example, the narrator finds himself objectified by the woman's gaze: "je n'étais plus du tout gêné d'être regardé comme l'une d'entre les nécessités de l'existence d'une femme" (275). An evaluation of Duras' views of homosexual men, however—a major focus in both her life and her art, especially since meeting her present companion, Yann Andréa—demonstrates how twisted her views of male (homo)sexuality can be.

In her discussion with Xavière Gauthier in May 1972, Duras advanced the following:

l'homosexualité, en tant que donnée naturelle, n'existe pas, bien sûr [. . .]. Il y a toujours eu, au départ de l'homosexualité masculine, un accident qui a fait que la voie, la voie de l'hétérosexualité a été abandonnée, hein, toujours [. . .] l'accident est un trauma de l'enfance, c'est sûr. (28)

She never repudiates such ludicrous notions of sexual pathology, yet nevertheless associates her own feelings as a woman with those of homosexual men (in her rejection of heterosexual men). Women, she feels, are in solidarity with homosexual men as persons who live "sur un fond de désespoir et de peur qui les ouvre" (152). As the section of La Vie matérielle entitled "Les hommes" shows, Duras maintains not only odd notions of homosexuality (cf. 46), but a very problematic vision of the heterosexual couple. Her insistent focus on the union formed by a heterosexual woman and a homosexual man in her recent fiction (Les Yeux bleus cheveux noirs, Emily L.)—often with an absent male to make a triangle—differs from her preoccupation with the heterosexual couple in her earlier fiction in which we find such ultimately banal representations of jealousy and adultery as shown in Dix heures et demie du soir en été, Le Ravissement de Lol V. Stein, and Hiroshima mon amour. In the newer duo which predominates, Duras not only maintains but reinforces the barriers to communication. Renaud Camus, reading La Maladie de la mort, shows how the author can attribute "sickness" to a male protagonist (whom Camus correctly reads, in this case, as homosexual) not simply because he does not love, but because he does not love women (72).

Duras dates her acquaintance with Yann Andréa to January 1980 (La Vie matérielle 142). First published in Libération and later in a collected volume,

L'Eté 80 traces the early development of the Duras/Andréa relationship by means of a progressively visible "vous" addressee and through the description of an 18-year old summer camp monitor (a young woman) and a very quiet, grey-eyed six-year old boy. Duras compares this textual relationship to that of herself and Andréa, the implied addressee of this text dedicated to him: "Comme eux nous sommes séparés" (93). In *L'Eté 80*, the barrier is simply that of age; the proposed reunion, in twelve years, would leave an entirely different set of circumstances for a 30-year old woman and an 18-year old man. The masochistic love represented in many of Duras' texts, like that of the suffering Chinese lover, is present "entre elle et lui"; between a woman and a child. As with Duras' homosexual companion, this impossible relationship is "désespérée": "cette douleur-là [. . .] le tourment invivable de ce désir-là" (85).

Les Yeux bleus cheveux noirs is also dedicated to Andréa. It was released at about the same time as *La Pute de la côte normande*. In this latter, shorter piece, Duras speaks of her relationship with Andréa in the summer of 1986 when she was (coincidentally) writing a stage scenario of *La Maladie de la mort* at her home in Neauphle-le-Château. Andréa would type under Duras' dictation, scream at her or at the world, and go out carousing:

> Il allait dans tous les sens, dans tous ces hôtels, pour chercher au-delà des hommes beaux, des barmen, des grands barmen natifs de la terre étrangère, celle d'Argentine ou de Cuba. Il allait dans tous les sens. Yann. (19)

He would return home to Marguerite and scream some more. Duras uses similar scenes of confrontation in her novels to expose the "walls" of separation

between major characters. She doesn't understand
Andréa's anger. He would say to her, for example:

> Qu'est-ce que vous foutez à écrire tout le temps, toute la
> journée? Vous êtes abandonnée par tous. Vous êtes folle,
> vous êtes la pute de la côte normande, une connarde, vous
> embarrassez. (16-17)

This is, of course, Duras' version. She has become
this "pute" by becoming a writer and, in this case, by
marketing a short piece (which, like *L'Eté 80*, originally appeared in *Libération*) in order to milk her
enormous public for her share of the 20-franc list
price. Many of Duras' characters are labelled whores:
the young French girl in Indochina (*L'Amant* 73),
Anna of *Le Marin de Gibraltar* (209, 316), the woman
of *La Maladie de la mort* (7), and others. As Hewitt
writes, Duras "flirts" in *L'Amant* not only with "the
scandalous assumption of feminine desire and passion
in a culturally and racially proscribed relationship,"
but also "with the idea of willful prostitution" (115).
In *La Pute de la côte normande*, Duras prostitutes the
Duras/Andréa relationship by her very *naming* of
Andréa, something not done in more "fictionalized"
versions such as *Les Yeux bleus cheveux noirs* or *Emily
L.* By publishing and embellishing details from her
private life in her novels, Duras also whorishly
"flirts" with the autofictive creation of her legend.
  While the Duras/Andréa relationship is mutually
beneficial, it is also destructive: "vivre comme ils
vivent, mieux vaut mourir" (*Les Yeux bleus cheveux
noirs* 194-95). Their books are a positive and pro-
ductive element of their relationship: "ce que nous
préférons, c'est écrire des livres l'un sur l'autre"
(*Emily L.* 61). The sexual barrier between them gives
the relationship its strength. The barrier of age and

sexual orientation is so conspicuous that it becomes part of each opposing side, an essential element of the inter-human communication. Duras' preferred relationships are as impossible as they are real: an "amour qui a tout pris et qui est impossible" (*Les Yeux bleus cheveux noirs* 134).

In the theatrical *Les Yeux bleus cheveux noirs*, the unnamed "Duras" woman, younger here, lies naked under the light of a bare bulb in a room near the sea: "Elle, encore contre le mur. Et lui encore la ramène vers le centre de l'attention, le lieu de la lumière théâtrale" (99). In the stark, seaside room, the violently harsh light shines upon the naked woman under the young man's gaze. But for the slow, hypnotic music, this scene recalls the close-up of Anne-Marie Stretter's sweating breast in the filmed version of *India Song*. The sea provides the background sound in *Les Yeux bleus cheveux noirs*, beating against the rocks behind which, in the invisible distance, lurks the Other (man), who is an object of both of the protagonists' empty passion and the subject of their discussion. Like the sea, he casts his presence into the house around which he prowls. As in *Emily L.*, where both man and woman equally desire the absent "Other," the homosexual man and heterosexual woman are drawn together by their mutual attraction to a third party. As Hewitt shows, Duras frequently introduces "a third term in the love rapport" to thus define "the self through the other's desire" (119). For the characters of the novel, this "third term" is a dark, blue-eyed man. For Duras and Andréa, it can also be their writings.

In much of her fiction, characters appear who exist "outside" the lives of principal protagonists, voyeurs who look in on the central figures, often through a window. Thus, in *Le Vice-consul* or its filmed version as *India Song*, just as we observe Anne-Marie Stretter in her Calcutta interior, so is she observed by the wandering crazy woman (upon whose outside world Anne-Marie Stretter can look, as well). Like the "you" of *L'Homme atlantique* (the man [Andréa] who moves on and off camera), principal characters step in and out of scenes they view through the windows which pierce the walls. Lol V. Stein looks in through a hotel room window which provides her with a partially obscured view of her old friend Tatiana Karl (making love with the novel's narrator). In *Emily L.* and *Les Yeux bleus cheveux noirs*, observers wander up to a hotel and lose their stance of objectivity when their lives become affected in reaction to what they see. Characters take on this role of witnesses ("la fameuse troisième personne," *M.D. à Montréal* 37), as will readers, becoming voyeurs peeking into the narrative framework.

When the man is not out chasing sex on the beach, the two characters of *Les Yeux bleus cheveux noirs* meet together to act out their inexplicable performance under the bare light bulb: it is a time for lies, tears, a certain *jouissance*, and uncomfortable tension. Together in the house, they each dream of this Other, the stranger with blue eyes and dark hair, the man they had seen as described in the first scene of the novel. By showing two protagonists both of whom direct their gaze upon the same man, Duras has chosen a couple whose shared passion for an absent Other creates between them an impossible love, beyond physicality, an ephemeral and yet permanent feeling which passes through them like the waves of the sea heard outside their room.

Duras transgresses barriers of gender and age to create this passion between an older, heterosexual woman (herself) and a younger, homosexual man (Yann Andréa). Andréa is Duras' late life Other, although, as she writes in *La Pute de la côte normande*, their love is formed with a built-in barrier:

> Il n'y avait rien dans ma vie qui avait été aussi illégal que notre histoire, qui n'avait pas cours ailleurs que là, là où nous étions. (18-19)

As seen in her film *Les Enfants*, social barriers such as age can be reconsidered with Duras. Societal barriers can also block development of the transgression of incest. Many of the most powerful relations in Duras' novels are incestuous. In *La Pluie d'été*, she will transcend taboo by clearly consummating the incestuous love. Duras' relationship with her younger brother who died in 1947, whether or not it was indeed physically passionate, is reflected in many of her "fictional" versions of siblings in *Agatha*, in *L'Amant*, in *Un Barrage contre le Pacifique* (Duras has said the character Joseph is her brother—*Les Lieux de Marguerite Duras* 46), and in the consummated episodes of *L'Amant de la Chine du Nord*. Like her alcoholism and her relationship with Andréa, Duras' incestuous biographical reality connects with her world of fiction.

Since Duras' love relationships are often a figuration of "l'amour impossible," the existing barriers make the passion which transcends them all the more powerful. She breaks down sociologically erected "walls" when her protagonists transgress not only conventional barriers of sexuality, but the ultimate separation of one human from another. She favors

35

relationships defined by real or figurative walls. Love which, by definition, is powerless and impotent produces a certain fruition nonetheless. The ultimate barrier (or wall) is that of the Other: the impossibility of transcending one's self even when there are no socially constructed boundaries. As Andréa writes to Duras, "Entre vous et moi, la séparation définitive: je vous aime" (121).

When Duras states in *L'Amant* that "L'histoire de ma vie n'existe pas" (14), she's lying, of course. Neither autobiography nor fiction, she does write her story; it is autofictive. Like the missing photograph of *L'Amant,* the autobiographical reality cannot be rendered into clear representation. In an interview with Bernard Pivot, she wonders what this curious enterprise of writing (*écriture*) is and why by means of it one would attempt this impossible doubling of one's self. Writing is a "filter," says Duras, which modifies and transforms reality; it is not an autobiographical mirroring: "c'est une sorte de désincrustation de l'expérience et même de l'imaginaire" (*M.D. à Montréal* 58). "*L'Amant* n'est pas un récit autobiographique," she says in another interview, "c'est une traduction" (*Le Monde*, 13 juin 1991). Through frequent public appearances, Duras' fiction is augmented by an autobiographical paratext which links the character portrait to that of herself: "Je vais de moi à moi. C'est ça le narcissisme" (ibid.). By rendering visible the constricting structure of her films and texts, she reminds us of the limitations of fictional representation. Her readers become voyeurs gazing through the narrative framework of the Durassian legend. She, Duras, willingly exhibits her persona as the paid storyteller, the *Pute de la côte normande.*

II

ELLE EST UNE AUTRE:
THE DUPLICITY OF SELF IN *L'AMANT*

Rachael Criso

> One creates from moment to moment
> and continuously the reality to which one
> gives a metaphoric name and shape, and
> that shape is one's own shape.
> (Olney 34)

> [. . .] "je" qui est Je et qui n'est pas
> toujours moi. (Proust quoted by Spitzer
> 418)

Marguerite Duras' *L'Amant* is a text ostensibly written as a first-person narrative, yet frequent shifts between the pronouns *je* and *elle* used to describe the narrator problematize our reading. The initial assumption may be that when the narrator refers to the subject as *elle*, she wishes to put distance between the more immediate *je* and a temporally or spatially removed self. However, upon closer observation the *je/elle* switches present themselves as more ambiguous.

Many critics consider *L'Amant* to be one of Duras' most directly autobiographical novels, especially in light of the recent publication of its sequel, *L'Amant de la Chine du Nord*. But can *L'Amant* be interpreted as pure autobiography, given the manner in which the narrator is portrayed from at least two angles, that is, from the first- and third-person narrative perspectives?

In her recent study of female autobiography, Leah Hewitt raises the question of "pronominal ambiguity" in *L'Amant*. Hewitt's work (*Autobiographical Tightropes*) concentrates on the autobiographical nature of the novel whose fragmented narrator she sees as a specifically gendered manifestation of a two-sided, active/passive, confessing self. The present essay deals with the subjective implication of the *je/elle* dichotomy. Attention here will not focus on the question of truth versus fiction, but explore instead a consciously split narrator who manipulates her narrative stance by the subtle interchange of two pronouns, challenging the reader to discover which facets of the narrator's psyche are revealed by each. Other complexities regarding the *je/elle* relationship will also be discussed, including the problematics of autobiographical assumptions as they pertain to *je/elle* usage, and the implications of the dual pronouns in connection with the constitution of an author/narrator through a self-recognized obsession with writing.

Despite *L'Amant*'s fragmentary nature, it is possible to reconstruct the story's chronology with some degree of accuracy. A large part of the narrative is retrospective, with commentary influenced by hindsight. Although in the past, events are articulated by use of many present, future and conditional tense verbs. The narrative concerns a young girl—possibly Duras, she is given no name—who meets an older Chinese man while living in a French colony in Indochina. He becomes her lover until she leaves for France, with apparently little regret. Many years later, the Chinese man contacts her and simply admits that he still loves her. Throughout the text, there are descriptions of the complicated relationship between the narrator and her family, her awakening sexuality and her constant concern with writing.

It is possible that the entire novel is fiction, or that it is detailed autobiography. More likely, it constitutes a subtle blending of the two. In her critical study, *Imagining a Self*, Patricia Meyer Spacks writes:

> It can be argued that all fiction (and poetry and philosophy and painting) ultimately constitutes autobiography, the artist inventing, whatever the purported aim of his creation, only a series of metaphors for the self. Conversely, one can maintain that all autobiography is fiction, the imposition of form and the discovery of meaning automatically converting life into its imitation. (154)

In this light, *je* and *elle* in *L'Amant* may both be understood as fictional and non-fictional, as representatives of an at once individual and universal subject. Why then the use of both the first- and third-persons: the differentiation between *je* and *elle*? A possible answer could come from Leo Spitzer who explains the widely accepted distinction between a "poetic I" and an "empirical I." The classic example he gives is the duality of Dante the protagonist and Dante the poet in *The Divine Comedy*. Spitzer suggests that in the medium of the "empirical I," the involvement is not at the level of biography, but concerns Dante's recognition of his own complicity with the human condition (416-18). Could we then describe the *je* in *L'Amant* as the "poetic I" and the *elle* as the "empirical I"? Perhaps.

When Rimbaud writes in the "Lettre du voyant" of May 1871, "Je est un autre" (Carré 39), he seems to be suggesting that the *je* in his poems has assumed its own identity, that the poet is fulfilling the role of a *voyant*, with privileged insight. Although Duras does not claim to be a visionary, a parallel may be drawn between her use of *je/elle* and Rimbaud's allusion to *je* and *autre*. A similar parallel is evident in the subject/Other distinction of psychoanalysis. The *je/elle* signifiers in *L'Amant* could be seen to denote two aspects of the psyche. Lacan believes that the subject is determined (that is, formed into a functioning and "normal" being) by the speech act which presupposes identification of an Other. Is it possible that the *elle* subject in *L'Amant* represents this subject as Other; that the third-person pronoun *spoken about* is adopted by the narrator when she intends, paradoxically, a more honest presentation of the *je*?

Another possible parallel for the subject(s) in *L'Amant* may be found in Jonathan Swift. To represent his public self in his journals, he refers to "I" or "t'other I," but when writing of his inner, private self, he calls it "Pdfr" (which probably stands for "Poor Dear Foolish Rogue"). Using this "little language," he converses with himself in his journal, playing the roles of both public and private self:[1]

> Answer M.D.'s [not Marguerite Duras'!] letter, Pdfr, 'ye hear? No says Pdfr, I won't yet, I'm busy: you're a saucy rogue. Who talks? (*Journal to Stella* 1:344)

This role-playing, or adaptation of a second persona in addition to *je*, closely resembles the *je/elle* dichotomy in *L'Amant*. In her text, Duras is aware of

---

[1] Discussed at length in *The Literary Persona* 158-63.

the duality of the narrator's personality. However, the question remains: which facet is presented by *je* and which by *elle*? Is it as in Swift, where *je* would be the public self on show, and *elle* the Pdfr model? Or is it the *elle* that is the public and *je* that is the private self?

As suggested above, some readers believe that the *elle* of the third-person narrative is used to distance the narrator from the narratee, breaking down the close relationship usually denoted by the use of *je*, as the third-person stance denies an intimate tone of complicity or confession—thus pushing further away the immediate likelihood of autobiography. *Elle*, for many, implies a forced distance, a non-committal attitude on the part of the narrator who, despite the fact that she is referring to herself, uses a displaced pronoun. Consequently, for these readers, the narrator appears to be closer to the narratee when the complicit *je* is used. However, the possibility exists that Duras' use of *elle* is more intimate than her use of *je*. It may be suggested that with the adoption of *elle*, the narrator reveals her hidden emotions, which are suppressed when *je* is used. Wherever *elle* appears, the mask of the *je*, public self, is cast aside and a private representation of the narrator is offered.

The narrator's use of *elle* when alluding to herself in passages concerning her lover and her mother is interesting. It appears to reveal an intimacy which more openly reflects her emotions, and, consequently, may be considered autobiographical. The lover is invariably referred to in the third person ("l'homme élégant," "lui," "l'homme de Cholen," "l'amant," "un homme," "l'homme," "mon amant," "Le Chinois de Cholen") and is never named. This apparent distancing initially causes the narratee to believe that the girl does not care for her lover. However, the first time they meet, a third-person narrative stance is adopted:

> Il vient vers elle lentement [. . .]. Tout d'abord il lui offre une cigarette [. . .]. Elle dit qu'elle ne fume pas [. . .]. Il lui dit que le chapeau lui va bien. (42)

The third-person is also used to describe the scene in which they sleep together for the first time. The choice of the present tense in this scene suggests a vivid memory and acute immediacy. By adopting the *elle* persona, the narrator is able to portray to the reader her true self, rather than the unfeeling personality she presents to her family. Also, in the passages where *elle* is used, the narrator does not have to face the *je* constituting her present self which contains all the knowledge and experience gained over the years. She simply sees herself as *elle*, exactly as she was then:

> Il fait sombre dans le studio, elle ne demande pas qu'il ouvre les persiennes. Elle est sans sentiment très défini. Elle éprouve une légère peur [. . .]. Lui, il tremble. Il la regarde tout d'abord comme s'il attendait qu'elle parle. Alors il ne bouge pas non plus, il ne la déshabille pas. (48-49)

The narrator abandons the impersonal *je* for this intimate and awkward scene to reveal her young, confused emotions:

> Elle ne le regarde pas. Elle le touche. Elle touche la douceur de son sexe, de la peau, elle caresse la couleur dorée, l'inconnue nouveauté. Il gémit, il pleure. Il est dans un amour abominable. (50)

Here, she displaces the third-person onto the lover. The use of *elle* suggests a closeness with him: they are both in the third-person and both removed from the harsher, public *je*: "Il l'accompagne à la pension. Elle descend, elle court, elle ne se retourne pas sur lui" (86). The use of *elle* may be an attempt to suppress the realization of her intense emotions. The depth of her relationship with her lover slowly becomes apparent and the use of the third-person retains its ambiguous role of seemingly distancing, yet ultimately revealing, a deep and sincere passion which will prove to be lasting. The narrator comments:

> L'amant de Cholen s'est fait à l'adolescence de la petite blanche jusqu'à s'y prendre. La jouissance qu'il prend à elle chaque soir a engagé son temps, sa vie. Il la regarde. Les yeux fermés il la regarde encore. Il respire son visage. (121)

The narratee is given an initial indication of her true feelings when the girl is on the boat about to leave for France:

> Elle aussi c'était lorsque le bateau avait lancé son premier adieu [. . .] qu'elle avait pleuré. Elle l'avait fait sans montrer ses larmes, parce qu'il était chinois [. . .]. Sa grande automobile était là [. . .]. Elle était un peu à l'écart [. . .]. C'était lui à l'arrière, cette forme à peine visible, qui ne faisait aucun mouvement terrassé. (136)

Later, while still on the boat, the full realization of her love overwhelms her. She admits the truth to herself, making a move as if to go and throw herself into the water:

43

Et la jeune fille s'était dressée comme pour aller à son tour se tuer, se jeter à son tour dans la mer et après elle avait pleuré parce qu'elle avait pensé à cet homme de Cholen et elle n'avait pas été sûre tout à coup de ne pas l'avoir aimé d'un amour qu'elle n'avait pas vu parce qu'il s''était perdu dans l'histoire comme l'eau dans le sable et qu'elle retrouvait seulement maintenant à cet instant de la musique jetée à travers la mer. (138)

In hindsight, the narrator appears completely detached from these events. The use of *elle* allows her a frankness that she is not able to express with *je*. At this key moment in the text the narratee knows for sure that the relationship is more serious than previously implied. The use of *elle* at this juncture is significant and underscores the likelihood that the third-person pronoun reveals more about the true feelings of the narrator than she is willing, or able, to express as "I."

The climax of this realization is recounted on the last page of the novel. The narrator has been contacted by the lover many years later. He telephones her and immediately a third-person stance is adopted: "Il lui avait téléphoné. Elle l'avait reconnu dès la voix" (41). And ultimately, "Il lui avait dit que c'était comme avant, qu'il l'aimait encore, qu'il ne pourrait jamais cesser de l'aimer, qu'il l'aimerait jusqu'à sa mort" (142). Despite the lapse of time and the separation, the intensity of their relationship has remained intact; and the narrator, as *elle*, can express this revelation.

With regard to the mother, the speaker uses both first- and third-person narrative. Their stormy relationship is obvious, as are the girl's ambiguous feelings toward her mother. This ambiguity is prevalent in the first-person sequences: "Je dis que je ne pourrais encore quitter ma mère sans en mourir de peine" (52). And, again, "Je lui dis que de ma mère une fois je me séparerai, que même pour ma mère, une fois je n'aurai plus d'amour" (58). However, a deeper resentment is embedded in the sections that use the third-person and suggest an autobiographical reading. The narrator, like Duras, resents her mother, indicates her madness, suggests she was not really a "good" mother. Perhaps the novel *L'Amant* was, among other things, a way for Duras to voice repressed but very real resentment toward the now-deceased mother. At one point in the text she admits:

> J'ai beaucoup écrit de ces gens de ma famille, mais tandis que je le faisais ils vivaient encore, la mère et les frères, et j'ai écrit autour d'eux, autour de ces choses sans aller jusqu'à elles. (14)

Of course, this is a narrator's voice, but an autobiographical honesty could easily be inferred, especially given the inclusion of some third-person references: *la mère, les frères*—as if she could not say *ma mère, mes frères*, which one would expect from the initial use of *je*. Was Duras perhaps afraid that the fictional veil would become too transparent? "C'est pour cette raison, elle ne le sait pas, que la mère permet à son enfant de sortir dans cette tenue d'enfant prostituée"(33). The apparently impersonal tone separates the speaker from emotions she displaces onto a third party. *Elle* is superficially used to repress, but in fact serves only to highlight, the difficult and perhaps autobiographical mother/daughter relationship:

45

> Je crois que du seul enfant aîné ma mère disait: mon
> enfant. Elle l'appelait quelquefois de cette façon. Des deux
> autres elle disait: les plus jeunes. (75)

Although this sentence begins with *je*, the third-person is quickly adopted with "des deux autres." The narrator removes herself, *je*, from the picture and substitutes the anonymous third-person reference. When the mother angrily questions her daughter about the extent of her relationship with the Chinese lover, the older brother encourages the mother to hit her: "[. . .] le frère répond à la mère, il lui dit qu'elle a raison de battre l'enfant" (73). The adoption of the third-person and the omission of the possessive adjectives suggest the exclusion felt by the narrator from her own family and the reference here to *la mère* indicates the narrator's imitation of her mother's refusal to use possessives. The narratee is given a privileged viewpoint, and the apparently distancing pronouns reveal the deeper feelings of jealousy and resentment. Yet, given the complexities of the mother/daughter relationship, the speaker still wants to please her mother, still wishes to see her happy, expressing this desire in the third-person:

> Et de ce dégoût aussi qu'elle pense à sa mère et que
> subitement elle crie et pleure de colère à l'idée de ne pas
> pouvoir changer les choses, faire la mère heureuse avant
> qu'elle meure. (123)

The impossibility of this enterprise is suggested by her previous descriptions of the mother's personality. It is a vain and futile hope which, given its failed resolution in the novel, could reflect Duras' autobiographical dilemma.

It is interesting to note the name of the narrator's friend, Hélène Lagonelle, and its repetition. The name contains the pronoun "elle" (Lagon*elle*), and the letter "l" appears four times. This character, who sexually intrigues the narrator, may be seen as the representative of her innocent self in awe of Hélène's body and mesmerized by her innocence, often comparing her own sexual knowledge to Hélène's chasteness.[2] The name is playfully repeated, and because of the way in which the narrator refers to herself as *elle* in the text, the *elle* contained in her friend's name mirrors the narrator's—as if despite the obvious differences, H.L. represented some part of the intimate side of the narrator/author herself:[3]

> Hélène Lagonelle ne va pas au lycée. Elle ne sait pas aller à l'école, Hélène L. Elle n'apprend pas [. . .]. Elle ne sait pas qu'elle est très belle, Hélène, L. [. . .]. Elle. Hélène L. Hélène Lagonelle [. . .]. Hélène Lagonelle, elle, elle ne sait pas encore ce que je sais. Elle, elle a pourtant dix-sept ans. (90-91)

The manner in which the narrator names herself in the text is likewise noteworthy. Not only does she use *je* and *elle*, but also: "cette enfant," "la petite," "l'enfant," "cette petite fille," "la première," "cette enfant-ci," "celle-ci," "enfant prostituée," "cette petite-là," "la petite prostituée blanche," "la petite

---

2 Could Duras also have heard in her friend's name the αγονια of the unfruitful, barren, or the not yet born, hence, chaste? Editor's note.

3 This abbreviated name of "L." to suggest the pronoun *elle* is also used by Duras in *Emily L.*, novel and protagonist. The "L" is again echoed in the character of Robert L. in *La Douleur*.

fille," "la petite fille blanche," "la pauvre enfant," "cette petite vicieuse." The articulation of these terms is often attributed to the mother or given as the terminology used by neighbors and gossipers. However, the fact that the narrator uses this abundance of "signifiants" to indicate one "signifié(e)" reflects her own perception of her divided self. These third-person designations are used throughout the text to aid the reader in the construction of an image of the speaker. The result is not uni-dimensional: *je*, from the point of view of the retrospective writer, but *elle*, the one seen by the mother, by the onlookers and the introspectively critical and honest, older narrator.

Throughout the text, there are numerous references to the writing process. The young narrator informs everyone around her that she will become a writer one day. She is not shy or hesitant, but sure and confident in her affirmation of this belief. Her mother tries to redirect her talents, but does not succeed. Each time the narrator mentions a literary career, she refers to herself as *je*. This is the retrospective author writing from the privileged standpoint of achievement. She knows, as we do, that she has indeed written several books: "Des années après la guerre, après les mariages, les enfants, les divorces, les livres [. . .] " (141). Throughout the text, she traces the development of her passion for writing and refers to herself as *je*; not the young aspiring *elle*, but the *je* who is sure of what she wants and sure that she will achieve it: "Je veux écrire. Déjà je l'ai dit à ma mère: ce que je veux c'est ça, écrire [. . .]" (29); and also, "Je lui ai répondu que ce que je voulais avant toute autre chose c'était d'écrire, rien d'autre que ça, rien [. . .] " (31). For the narrator, to write is as natural as breathing—it

does not hold the complications of human relationships, even though both writing and love are essentially beyond reach:

> Je n'ai jamais écrit, croyant le faire, je n'ai jamais aimé,
> croyant aimer, je n'ai jamais rien fait qu'attendre devant la
> porte fermée. (34)

In literary production, the narrator discovers that she
is capable of controlling and ordering her emotions.
For example, when writing about her mother, she
says: "C'est pourquoi j'en écris si facilement d'elle
maintenant, si long, si étiré, elle est devenue écriture
courante" (38). The *elle* is unable to understand certain conflicting emotions, but the *je* of experience
takes control and through cathartic writing succeeds
in coming to terms with the confusion experienced by
the younger *elle*.

The autobiographical implications of the gradual
constitution of an author are evident. The narrator
deliberately builds up a picture of a developing writer
who could clearly be Duras herself. We know that
Duras felt the compulsion to write early in life, and
for the retrospective reader, the *je* and *elle* could easily
be interpreted as autobiographical representations of
conflicting sides of the emerging author.

Autobiographical or not, *L'Amant* presents two
separate subjects: *je* and *elle*, which denote a narrator
divided into two distinct selves. Both pronouns appear in the past tense narration of events, so it cannot
be assumed that *je* constitutes a time present and *elle*
a time past representation of the narrator. Both are
also used with regard to most events, so the shifts are
not dictated by the action. They represent, rather, an
intentional fragmentation into *je*—used to relate su-

perficial events and situations over which the narrator feels control (e.g., conversations with her family, and discussions of her writing)—and *elle*, used to illustrate difficult emotions, such as fear, frustration, jealousy, hate, resentment, and love. The narrator is able to express the latter more easily through a displacement of her own subject onto the third-person. The use of *elle* may seem more distant initially but, paradoxically, it conveys the more intense and psychologically revealing emotions. Stephan Shapiro writes:

> Truth in autobiography is not merely fact or conformity to "likeness," to the way one appears to others, but rather the projection of a story of successive self-images and recognitions or distortions of those self-images by the world; it is the story of idenity as the tension between self-image and social recognition. (426)

Self-image and social recognition are both elements which Duras had to consider carefully while writing *L'Amant de la Chine du Nord*. In many respects a re-write of *L'Amant*, the later work elaborates upon many nuanced and implied details of its predecessor. In an interview, Duras acknowledges the suggestion of autobiography in *L'Amant*, while maintaining that she does not aspire to document her life.[4] Despite this, a clear progression between the two novels is apparent. In the preface to the 1991 version Duras indicates that she wrote *L'Amant de la Chine du Nord* after learning of the death of her Chinese lover

---

4 Referring to Jacques Annaud's recent film based on *L'Amant* and his questionable interpretation, Duras says: "Il veut faire ma vie à travers *L'Amant*, une biographie filmée [. . .]. Il confond *L'Amant* avec un livre de souvenirs" (*Lire* 58).

(11-12), which, like the death of her mother, may have set her free.

Interestingly, the narrator in the later novel does not adhere to *L'Amant*'s duality; she is *l'enfant*, still in the third-person, but no longer pitted against an opposing *je*. This altered narrative perspective invites comparative speculation and further questioning of autobiographical intent. However, even without the crutch of assuming documented truth, this shift from multiple to single narrator represents a stabilizing acceptance of closure in a resolved relationship. The lover is dead—at last *je* and *elle* may be united to constitute a coherent narrator who dares finally to speak freely, and with one voice.

III

THE UNSPEAKABLE HEROINE OF *EMILY L.*

Julia Lauer-Chéenne

Many critics have related the role of silence in the Durassian universe to absence, the feminine, reading, and writing. In *Emily L.* the unspeakable opens into the impossible, a love story between a homosexual man and a heterosexual woman. Their story is told via two frames, one fictional, the other autobiographical. Both, enhanced by intertextual readings, interact and illustrate the coy slippage between fact and fiction similar to that of *L'Amant*, Duras' would-be autobiographical novel of 1984, and its rewriting in *L'Amant de la Chine du Nord*, 1991. The unspeakable in *Emily L.* refers not only to the richness of silence and to the inexplicable love bond, but to the nature of the heroine herself, a woman of unspeakable transgression.

Silence and Emptiness

Narration in *Emily L.* is inspired by the gap between representation and experience. The narrator and her male companion are at a café in Quillebeuf-sur-Seine. She expresses her desire to write about their love affair, but acknowledges the problems of doing so. In the background an English couple, the

Captain and Emily L., enact a love story the narrator eventually relates, not as a whole, but as fragments interrupted by observations, comments, and memories. As she speaks, the two stories become entwined so that paradoxically she tells and writes the impossible tale.

In *Emily L.* the difficulty of writing, speaking, and defining the love relationship is presented overtly. The narrator disclaims the possibility of ever capturing it: "Notre histoire, elle ne sera nulle part, elle ne sera jamais tout à fait écrite" (55). Her companion denies its existence: "Il n'y a rien à raconter. Rien" (23). The incommunicable love story is a boundary toward which the text strives, a goal that escapes translation. The narrator's only solution is to present the *histoire* indirectly: "Non [. . .] ce que j'écris en ce moment, c'est autre chose dans quoi elle serait incluse, perdue, quelque chose de beaucoup plus large peut-être [. . .]. Mais elle, directement, non, c'est fini [. . .] je ne pourrai plus [. . .]" (22-23).

Silence and emptiness, leitmotifs that contradict the printed page's traditional authority which "tends toward a spatially arrested and visible, hence 'real' permanence" (Suda 9), are accentuated in *Emily L.* Duras has often affirmed that for her, writing is process and discovery: "Je ne sais jamais très bien où je vais; si je savais, je n'écrirais pas, puisque c'est fait, ce serait fait" (Duras and Porte 37). Furthermore, Duras distrusts categorical statements: "Je fuis ceux des gens qui au sortir d'apprendre les choses ou de les voir savent déjà penser, et quoi, et quoi dire, et comment conclure" (*L'Eté 80* 46). In *Emily L.* this uneasiness translates into linguistic malaise and silence that subvert any attempt to fix meaning. The protagonists cannot articulate their most profound feelings for one another. The French couple is unable to name (*nommer*) their fascination for the Captain and Emily L. (31), nor can they verbalize why they are so enchanted with Quillebeuf. The narrator's fear is inborn "sans langage pour se dire" (51); in her love letter Emily L. speaks "dans l'oubli des mots" (135). The protagonists do not tell of some of their most significant actions: the Captain never admits he burned his wife's poem; Emily L. and the notary never speak of their joint effort to reach the young caretaker.

Nonverbal communication comes closer to grasping underlying truths. In the love scene with the caretaker, Emily L. struggles with words as their eyes meet in mute understanding:

> —J'aurais voulu vous dire une chose afin que ce soit dit [. . .] mais je suis empêchée de le faire [. . .].
> —Une chose que vous n'avez jamais dite?
> —Jamais. Mais ce n'est pas la peine. Vous savez cette chose aussi bien que je la sais. (117)

Their love is symbolized by one static kiss, similar to the kisses in *Moderato cantabile* and *Les Yeux bleus cheveux noirs* in which all is spent in a single, immobile moment. The love affair never consummated, never written, never spoken, exists only as an unoccupied place, described in Emily L.'s letter:

> Je voulais vous dire ce que je crois, c'est qu'il fallait toujours garder par devers soi, voici, je retrouve le mot, un endroit, une sorte d'endroit personnel, c'est ça pour y être seul et pour aimer. Pour aimer on ne sait pas quoi, ni qui ni comment, ni combien de temps. Pour aimer, voici que tous les mots me reviennent tout à coup [. . .] pour garder en soi la place d'une attente, on ne sait jamais, de l'attente d'un amour, sans encore personne peut-être, mais de cela et seulement de cela, de l'amour. (135)

Unable to define or describe this inner space, Emily L. can only refer to it as a formless passage or as a threshold of potential, a reflection of the relationship between the narrator and her companion: "Nous ne pouvions mentir en rien sur ce sentiment qui nous avait unis et nous unissait encore sans doute, mais dont nous ne parlions plus jamais" (48).

Emptiness, like silence, is seized in *Emily L.* as an opportunity for imaginative interpretation. Closing one's eyes or looking without seeing evokes the mind's eye of imagination, the vacant look of the unconscious, what Anton Ehrenzweig refers to as "the open-eyed empty stare" (107). The *nonregard* is linked to rêverie and emptiness essential for creativity. Gazing is prevalent in *Emily L.*, a means of both erasure and projection. Emily L. looks at the floor and closes her eyes, similar to other self-forgetful heroines of Duras' œuvre. The narrator's companion loses himself in daydreams: "Vous avez regardé dehors, vers le fleuve, sans voir, rien, longtemps, méfiant" (21). Gazing without seeing is an escape from the moment at hand, a way to ponder and let the mind roam: "De nouveau nous regardons au-delà du propos, du moment. Nous regardons le fleuve, la place, l'été qui dort" (57). The Captain's look at Emily is likened to the visualization of emptiness itself: "Il reste les yeux baissés longtemps, puis tout à coup il la regarde longuement comme on le ferait d'un paysage bouleversant et insaisissable, celui du vide de la mer ou celui du vide d'un ciel" (94). Duras frequently makes use of indistinct landscapes (particularly oceans, fogs, and skies) to evoke the state of pure vision.[1] The stark, white cliffs of the Quillebeuf region mirror the silent, blank page vital to the creative process: "Blanc serait la couleur d'un silence absolu regorgeant de possibilités; le silence d'une pensée cachée qui précède tout commencement" (Michel 13-14). The white railing along the river extends the metaphor of writing on the landscape:

> Vous avez dit que le fleuve était quadrillé et retenu par la grille de ce bastingage—les eaux bleu-noir par le blanc lacté—comme le bleu par le blanc dans les dernières peintures de Nicolas de Staël. (63)

Alternating black and white images suggest the passage between what has been written and what has not, recalling the reference to "les régions claires" and "les régions obscures" in L'Amant.[2] Emily L. writes with a black pen on white paper kept in a black dossier. The roads to Quillebeuf alternate between darkness and light. The unfinished poem is described in terms of written and crossed out portions:

> Le Captain avait lu le poème à travers les ratures et les régions claires de l'écriture. Cette région-là lui paraissait plus étrangère que celles dont elle avait douté. Elle disait à travers les ratures que certains après-midi d'hiver les rais de soleil qui s'infiltraient dans les nefs des cathédrales oppressaient de même que les retombées sonores des grandes orgues.

---

[1] Gaston Bachelard describes this state in L'Air et les songes: "L'être méditant s'y trouve devant une phénominalité minima, qu'il peut encore décolorer, atténuer, qu'il peut effacer" (194-5).

[2] Duras has often linked the color black, associated with death, the hidden, and the repressed, to the scene of writing. See "l'ombre interne" (Les Parleuses 50), "la chambre noire" (ibid. 191), and "le bloc noir" (La Vie matérielle 30).

Dans les régions claires de l'écriture elle disait que les blessures que nous faisaient ces mêmes épées de soleil nous étaient infligées par le ciel. (84-85)

In the Durassian universe silence, rêverie, and blank spaces are privileged as means by which exteriority may be suspended and erased, thereby awakening transcendent awareness. In this light, the narrator's reaction to the Koreans can be attributed to an anxiety born from occupied space that should be empty:

C'est entre deux arrivées du bac, dans ce vide de la place, que la peur est arrivée. Je regarde autour de nous et voici qu'il y a des gens, là-bas, au fond de cette place, à la sortie du chemin abandonné, là où il ne devrait y avoir personne. (11)

Filling this gap involves transgressing into the suppressed, and the hidden, a journey accompanied by fear of writing the inexpressibly objectionable. Carol Murphy points out that it is the negated space of writing's erasure through metaphoric displacement that will render the story legendary (*Neophilologus* 541). This erasure, performed through the play of entwined tales in *Emily L.*, makes possible the shifts between told and untold stories and between the fictional heroine and Duras herself, the indirect subject of the text.

Doubling

Contrasted with the nonlook of rêverie is a gaze that projects, doubles, and fascinates. It is evident in the initial view of the Captain and Emily L.: "Nous avions dû les regarder sans les voir et puis brusquement les voir. Pour ne plus jamais ensuite pouvoir

faire autrement" (16). An informed reader participates in the gaze of fascination, recognizing similarities among Duras, the narrator, and Emily L. that
hint at the love story's indirect representation. Both
Emily L. and Marguerite Duras are elderly, petite
women in frail health, older than their male compan-
ions, writers with pseudonyms,[3] and somewhat eccen-
tric. Duras has confirmed the resemblance in a
television interview: "Ma parente profonde, ma
sœur, c'est Emily L. C'est moi, à un point que vous
ne pouvez imaginer."[4] Both women have lost a child,
are estranged from their blood relatives, and have ap-
proached the edge of madness. In addition, various
allusions to Duras' personal history (alcoholism, a
blond-haired companion, a childhood in Indochina,
an apartment in Normandy, a writing career) inten-
sify the autobiographical tone of *Emily L.* The
narrator voices opinions similar to Duras', particularly on the subject of writing.

Mirrors and reflections are a hallmark of the
Durassian œuvre which Michèle Druon links with two
other elements: the absence of the originary moment
of suffering, and—once the double is found—an appeasement of suffering via a *ravissement* of self-
dispossession (95). These observations apply to the
narrator in *Emily L.* who, unable to stipulate the
source of her anxiety, projects it onto her surroundings

---

[3] For a commentary on the change from Donnadieu to Duras see
Aliette Armel, *Marguerite Duras et l'autobiographie* 143-44. The
homonym in Emily L. (*elle*) increases the play between *je* and *elle*
also found in *L'Amant* and constitutes a further subversion of the
patronymic.

[4] "Marguerite Duras," prod. Luce Perrot, TF1 June 26-July 17, 1988.
Quoted by Armel 125.

in a variety of ways. Doubling is apparent from the outset, when fear is inspired by a group of Koreans who appear to be "une même personne indéfiniment multipliée" (11). The effect continues with the troubling episode reminiscent of hallucinations Duras suffered during her period of alcoholic detoxification: "Vous aussi vous aviez peur que recommencent à se montrer à moi ces choses de la nuit" (12). The narrator states her presence as object of the gaze, like Emily L.: "Moi, la femme de ce récit, celle qui est à Quillebeuf cet après-midi avec vous, cet homme qui me regarde [. . .]" (14). There is a mirror behind the bar in which the Captain views the narrator and her companion. The young manageress resembles her mother; the conversation at times is *doublée* in French and English.

Similarities between the French and English couples multiply the doublings. Despair is common to both. About the English couple the narrator says: "Ça se voyait que c'était fini et en même temps qu'elle était là encore" (20), recalling the *histoire* between the narrator and her companion, "celle qui était encore là et qui n'en finissait pas de mourir" (21). A deep bond unites the couples even though love appears to be waning. Emily L. depends on the Captain for her very life: "Que s'il était parti d'elle, elle serait morte là où il l'aurait quittée, ça se voyait aussi" (20). The Captain refuses to survive alone: "Il ne veut pas qu'elle meure, lui, il lui interdit de mourir, en quelque sorte, pour cette raison-ci que lui ne veut pas de sa mort à elle dans sa vie à lui, pas de ça jamais" (100). There exists a similar reciprocity in *La Vie matérielle* where Duras describes her relationship with Yann Andréa:

> Il a cette volonté enfantine de me faire manger pour que je
> ne meure pas, il ne veut pas que je meure mais il ne veut
> pas que je grossisse non plus, c'est difficile à concilier et
> moi, je ne veux pas qu'il meure non plus, notre
> attachement c'est ça, notre amour. (144)

The unnamed point of intersection between doubles in *Emily L.* leads into the unspoken core of the text. The essence of the destroyed poem is the heart of all matter, "celle, interne, au centre des significations" and, like the untold love story, is "ailleurs et loin de là où on aurait pu croire" (85). This follows the Durassian tradition of displaced or missing signifiers, such as the victim's head in *L'Amante anglaise*, the lost photograph in *L'Amant*, and the absence of the look of blue eyes in *Les Yeux bleus cheveux noirs*. This missing center relates to absence and silence, "le centre de ce qui n'a pas de centre, le Silence absolu, primordial et dernier" (Michel 62) and translates into decentered writing of the unspeakable.

Transgression

At the absent heart of *Emily L.* is the elusive love story between Duras and Yann Andréa, one that remains private but not secret. It is public knowledge that the couple are not only professional collaborators, but live together as close friends. It may have been the publication of *M.D.*, Andréa's personal account of Duras' detoxification, that inspired Duras to write *L'Amant*. In *Emily L.*, the link to Andréa is deliberately implied, as it is in other works, such as *L'Homme atlantique, La Maladie de la mort, Les Yeux bleus cheveux noirs*, and *La Pute de la côte normande*, works Armel has called "le cycle Yann Andréa" (97-126).

These facts are relevant because of the close connection between Duras' personal life and her œuvre which numerous critics have analyzed.[5] Passion and desire, major elements in Duras' fiction, have a counterpart in fact. Armel quotes from a televised interview with Luce Perrot in which Duras confirms the link between passion and writing: "La chose devant laquelle je n'ai jamais reculé, ce sont les expériences passionnelles. Elles étaient aussi fortes que les livres et se posaient en termes d'urgence. Les livres peut-être pouvaient attendre, mais pas le désir, la passion" (100). Duras continues in the same interview, confessing her own unfaithfulness and attesting to the twin therapies of writing and passion: "Ce qui m'a sauvée, c'est que je trompais les hommes avec lesquels je vivais. J'aimais l'amour, j'aimais aimer. Avec écrire ça sauvait."

Violence and madness, other Durassian leitmotifs, may be elucidated by nonfictional connections. At the age of about twelve, the author experienced simultaneously her first menstrual period and an overwhelming desire to murder her family:

> C'est sans doute à cette époque-là que j'ai approché le plus de la folie. Je crois que pendant un mois j'étais réveillée, toujours par les mêmes rêves, des rêves meurtriers, je voulais tuer ceux que j'aimais le plus au monde, c'est-à-dire mes frères et ma mère. Je voulais tuer tout. C'est une des périodes les plus difficiles de mon existence, parce que je n'osais pas le dire à ma mère. (Lamy 66)

---

5 See, for example, Aliette Armel, Jean Pierrot, Madeleine Borgomano. (And, most recently, Alain Vircondelet. Editor's note.)

This unspoken undercurrent seeps through in *Emily L.* where, as Murphy points out, the flow of the pen is situated within the menstrual flow: "A douze ans ça a dû être fait. J'ai laissé courir [. . .]" (*Emily L.* 58, Murphy 544). In the same way, the sexually promiscuous woman, a prevailing figure in the Durassian œuvre, may be traced to Duras' childhood. The author speaks of her fascination with Anne-Marie Stretter, a prominent figure of both her fiction and her youth:

> Je pense que c'était ça, elle, Anne-Marie Stretter, le modèle parental pour moi, le modèle maternel, ou plutôt le modèle féminin; elle ne m'apparaissait pas comme maternelle, elle était avant tout une femme adultère, voyez non pas la mère des petites filles. (Duras and Porte 65)

There is an almost magical appeal to adultery in Duras' texts in which infidelity is not a negative characteristic, but a necessity. In *Les Parleuses* she states that most women do not live a true sexual life because they are still trapped in "une peur moyenageuse de l'infidélité" (41). Emily L. joins with other Durassian heroines in transgressing the limits. In her husband's eyes, writing poetry places her in the category of unfaithful women:

> Tout comme si elle l'eût trahi, qu'elle eût eu une autre vie parallèle à celle qu'il ait crue être la sienne, ici, dans la maison des garages. Une vie clandestine, cachée, incompréhensible, honteuse peut-être, plus douloureuse encore pour le Captain que si elle lui avait été infidèle avec son corps—ce corps ayant été avant ces poèmes la chose du monde qui l'aurait fait sans doute la supprimer si elle l'avait donné à un autre homme. (78)

Coupled with the Captain's reaction is that of Emily L. who admits her own infidelity, not to her husband, but to the young caretaker: "Contrairement à toutes les apparences, je ne suis pas une femme qui se livre corps et âme à l'amour d'un seul être, fût-il celui qui lui est le plus cher au monde. Je suis quelqu'un d'infidèle" (135).

Literal prostitution in this text is replaced by a symbolic one which implicates Duras as narrator and author. Writing, sexuality, and self-forgetfulness go hand in hand.[6] Martha Evans states in her discussion of *Le Ravissement de Lol V. Stein* that the porous, indifferent nature of the heroine makes her "anonymous, exchangeable, the best whore of all" (151). By extension, she says, the book is passed around and exchanged in the manner of a whore and that the woman writer embodies a similar promiscuity, that is, that "women writers are indeed prostitutes standing forth with the indecent truth that we are all whores" (156). Evans cites an interview in which Duras insinuates that the book takes her place as a public, commercial, and somewhat obscene display:

> J'écris pour me déplacer de moi au livre. Pour m'alléger de mon importance. Que le livre en prenne à ma place. Pour me massacrer, me gâcher, m'abîmer dans la parturition du livre. Me vulgariser, me coucher dans la rue. (Schuster and Duras 179)

Yet, Duras' texts are not direct confessions of a life characterized by the author herself as indecent and scandalous. Although her œuvre encompasses fiction and nonfiction, it is poetic, not literal truth that defies

---

[6] See "Le corps des écrivains" in *La Vie matérielle*.

one universal reading. Liliane Papin attributes the poetical force of Duras' texts to the unspoken:

> Tous les "blancs," tous les "manques à voir" dont elle laisse le texte parsemé sont autant de creux où l'imagination s'engouffre, comme happée par la force du vide, où le langage se multiplie à l'infini, où ce qui est dit s'accompagne toujours du poids du "non-dit" en échos incessants, signe incontestable d'un langage poétique. (83)

Likewise, the stories of *Emily L.*, fragmented by digressions and descriptive passages, amplify silence via blanks filled by diverse readings and interpretations. The roads to Quillebeuf through marshes, streams, and dense forests are reminders of other Durassian settings: the woods of *Détruire dit-elle* and the waters in *Un Barrage contre le Pacifique, Le Vice-consul*, and *L'Amant*. These mirrored and entangled stories create a text that resists interpretation, one that splinters into subtexts that appear, disappear, and reappear, evoking Durassian silence, as she has defined it: "C'est ce que j'appelle le silence, c'est-à-dire des textes enchevêtrés, mélangés, qui ne vont dans aucune direction donnée, qui créent un instant que je dirais absolu de cinéma."[7] In *Emily L.* images become entwined so that there is not just one story but several, incomplete and related. Duras' past is evoked, since part of Quillebeuf's charm stems from the yellow sky of Siam, a memory of her childhood in Indochina. This provides another background from which to interpret the fear of the Koreans and the fascination of the ferry crossing. Quillebeuf is also part of the setting in *La*

---

[7] *Marguerite Duras à Montréal* 46. These remarks are made with regard to *India Song*, Duras' film version of *Le Vice-consul*.

Pute de la côte normande, a slim, autobiographical volume closely linked to *Les Yeux bleus cheveux noirs* and *La Maladie de la mort*.

The impossible love story's expansion into uncharted territory is accomplished through the negative space of the unsaid. The young manageress asks personal questions about the sea journey of the Captain and Emily L., blundering into the tension between the spoken and the unspoken which undermines a straightforward analysis of *Emily L.* Her transgression is linked to the *inter-dit* of multiple narrative regions and to the *interdit* beyond boundaries. The English couple's ocean trips, different from the sort imagined by the young woman, are like the text itself, fragmented into numerous discourses and lacunae which may never be fully saturated with meaning. This process of resistance "creuse un répit de l'écriture qui, dans le silence créé, s'accorde au 'diapason' du Silence, de l'Interdit" (Michel 129).

The narrator characterizes the guardrail along the water as "fragile et blanc" (9), "dérisoire en regard de sa fonction" (65), "un problème sans fin, sans fond" (63), thereby evoking an attempt to protect the text from expanding into infinite openness. Duras' *écriture courante* subverts the effort toward a projected aim, however, slipping between fiction and autobiography with the transgression of *je* and (Emily) *L*.

IV

LOSS, ABANDONMENT, AND LOVE: THE EGO IN EXILE

Marie-France Etienne

> Ecrire ce n'est pas raconter des histoires [. . .] c'est raconter une histoire et l'absence de cette histoire. C'est raconter une histoire qui en passe par son absence. (*La Vie matérielle* 31)

> Je me suis dit qu'on écrivait toujours sur le corps mort du monde, et, de même, sur le corps mort de l'amour. (*Ecrire dit-elle* 257)

The entire corpus of Marguerite Duras' texts presents a narrative of absence, a narrative of death. As Julia Kristeva points out, in Duras' work, "Death and pain are the spider's web of the text [. . .] " (*Black Sun* 229). Each text weaves a new design of the same story, and each is one step closer toward the center of an original which speaks of loss and abandonment. The same tale, told each time in a different text, in a different voice, re-enacts a primal forgotten scene.

With *Moderato cantabile*, 1958, Marguerite Duras for the first time writes from her silence, translating, as she says, "from the unknown," from an unspeakable darkness. Her writing confronts, in Kristeva's terms, "the silence of horror in oneself and in the world" (*Black Sun* 225). In *Moderato*, as in many of the works that follow, a man is the passive and fascinated observer of a woman's searching. She asks him for the words that will allow her to tell the story which defines her, which gives her form. In the texts prior to 1980, men hold the word, while women are possessed by images whose signifiers have been erased.[1]

The play on language and its absence, the unspeakability of the text, seem to have acquired a new dimension in Duras' latest works. In *La Maladie de la mort*, 1982, a turning point in her writing, the language of darkness, the language of silence, is inscribed in the woman's body which becomes "the fictive sign" par excellence, that is, the sign whose referent is imaginary. Fictive body, sign of an absence which carries the text of death within itself, she alone can read that text to the other. Woman, and more specifically here, her sex, is the knot where the symbolic and the imaginary are intertwined. The penetration of the feminine body is the entering of a text to be deciphered. To enter the body, to penetrate the silence of the text, is to enter the unrepresentable: death.

There is a universal link established between death and the "penis-lacking feminine." As Kristeva points out: "[T]he unrepresentable nature of death [is] linked with that other unrepresentable—original abode but also resting-place for dead souls, in the beyond which, for mythical thought, is constituted by the female body" (*Black Sun* 27). In *La Maladie de la mort*, the

---

[1] See my "L'Oubli et la répétition: *Hiroshima mon amour*," *Romanic Review* 78:4, 1987.

woman's sex becomes a metaphor for death and speaks of the irreplaceable loss of the mother: "The feeling of unavoidable abandonment [. . .] is formed about the maternal figure," Kristeva comments on *La Maladie de la mort* (ibid. 241). The man endlessly asks the woman to tell him the story of the child he was. She is in the place of the loss, embodies the lack. He is dying of the "malady of grief" not knowing "how to lose [. . .]. It follows that any loss entails the loss [. . .] of being itself" (ibid. 5). The loss of his being is read on her body; she speaks his death. "It is She who is death-bearing, therefore I do not kill myself in order to kill her but I attack her, harass her, represent her [. . .]" (ibid. 28). By endlessly looking at her body, by "speaking" it, forming and deforming it, he tries to represent what cannot be expressed: death. The penetration of her text, the reading of his, is linked to a dissolution of language, a dissolution of form, an effacing of the word into silence.

The narrative of silence, the unspeakability of the text, is again at the core of Duras' latest works: *La Pluie d'été*, 1990, and *L'Amant de la Chine du Nord,* 1991. More than any of her previous works, *La Pluie d'été* tells the story of the child, the pre-oedipal child who cannot name the loss of the abandoned, silent womb. In *Jours de l'an*, Hélène Cixous seems to give the reader of *La Pluie d'été* the entire sinuous structure of Duras' book. She writes: "Dans le ventre de la chambre il y a un livre dans le ventre duquel il y a un homme dans le ventre de laquelle il y a la musique dans le flot de laquelle l'enfant trouve la joie et la noyade, dans le ventre de laquelle tout à fait au fond, un corps se métamorphose en vers [. . .]" (182).[2] The creating spaces in *La Pluie d'été* are named: the kitchen, the bedroom in which the mother's love story is recalled for the first time, the *appentis*, the womb in which a book is found, the burned book which contains and tells the story of a man, the lost lover, the son Ernesto. This lost, silent lover, this beloved son is also, as we shall see, the mother who sings the song without words, "La Neva," the song of love and abandonment in which dwells the crying child in its multiple guises. In the sentence quoted from Cixous, the man becomes a feminine, maternal presence through the words, "un homme dans le ventre de *laquelle*." In Duras' text the same slippage of gender, of meanings, will occur, underlining the merging of the lover-son-mother. The metamorphosis of the word, language and its absence, will delineate the trajectory of love and abandonment.

In *La Pluie d'été*, Marguerite Duras tells us a story and "the absence of this story." The story is of a family: the father, the mother, and their many children: Ernesto, Jeanne, and the "brothers and sisters," who are designated in English, in a foreign language, reflecting the alienation of the family and more specifically of the exiled mother who has abandoned her native tongue. As in many of Duras' texts, the names of most of the characters fluctuate and some are nameless, an indication of the instability of their identities: "Deprived of meaning, deprived of values" (*Black Sun* 14), they wander about in a text

---

[2] The section titles of this essay: "Le Pays perdu" and "Le Pays venant" are borrowed from Hélène Cixous.

which emerges in the gaps between the words, in the "non-dit."

The dispossessed characters live on the outskirts of Paris, in a marginal way. The parents regularly go to the "centre-ville" to get drunk and find books that have been abandoned and in which they recognize their own story. From the start, the writing/reading of the story is thus linked to abandonment and loss. The characters evolve in a reality they "invent," "find" (*invenire*), in the written word of a text. Ernesto is the eldest. He is a genius and is not given any precise age: child or a man, one does not know for sure. His name has the same fluidity and vagueness as his age. He is the one who "knows" how to read and write without having been taught. He "reads" a book found by his brothers, a "livre brûlé" whose center is lacking, whose written story exists only as an absence. He invents (finds) the story through inventing (finding) the words, through incorporating its silence: "Dans les jours qui avaient suivi la découverte du livre brûlé Ernesto était entré dans une phase de silence" (*La Pluie* 13). Reading becomes the unfolding "dans son propre corps d'une histoire par soi inventée" (16). The story is contained within the body; the body of the child is the body of the text. The child *is* the text. The story which exists in the absence of the story (told by the child-text in the silence of the erased words) speaks of a loss, speaks of a lost love. It is contained within the body of another text, the mother-text: *La Pluie d'été*. The maternal body and the body of the child indistinguishably tell the same unspeakable story.

The text expressed in the writing/telling of a story "qui en passe par son absence" finds its locus in the metaphor of "le livre brûlé" and its appendix: "La

Neva," the maternal song without words, locations of abandonment and loss in which the characters are trapped. The silent core of the "livre brûlé," the silent words of "La Neva" represent "a [. . .] negation of that impossible loss" (*Black Sun* 91), the original one. The words have been erased because the loss cannot be named. The words of the "livre brûlé," invented words which give back its meaning to the story, the remembered words of "La Neva" will tell the impossible love, the love nested at the core of the loss, and through the wording, reconcile the love and the loss.

The ambivalence of the text is expressed through word-forms, spatial metaphors which shape this love/loss relationship, or through the blanks of discourse. At the center of language, at the center of silence dwell "le livre brûlé" and its double, "La Neva," the mother and the emptiness, the gap of meaning they contain at their core. To enter the word is to enter the lack, to enter the site of the unrepresentable, the ultimate loss.

The Lost Object of Love: *Le Pays perdu*

All the characters in *La Pluie d'été* are exiled beings that seem to function, speak and act from an empty space within. This undefined space, when it formulates itself, emerges as a vague language whose meaning lies elsewhere, in a silence either expressed literally (the word "silence" is quite often written), or suggested. Words, at the same time, tell and don't tell. The exiled woman has abandoned everything and has been abandoned by what she has left behind. In search of the "lost country," "the unspeakable," the foreigner is exiled to the self. A letting go, exile is also " [. . .] a way of gambling with death, which is the

71

meaning of life, of stubbornly refusing to give in to the law of death." One has to let go of a tongue to find one's own text, because "writing is impossible without some kind of exile." One must let go of hi-story to find the absent story: "For if meaning exists in the state of exile, it nevertheless finds no incarnation, and is ceaselessly produced and destroyed in geographical or discursive transformations" (*The Kristeva Reader* 298).

The Mother

The mother is here, as in many of Duras' texts, the most powerful figure. She is the center from which and around which the other characters evolve. All are her children, with the exception of the "instituteur," the outsider who wants to be included in the empty space delineated by the characters. The father himself is a child of hers, in his own eyes: "Aussi le père se désignait-il lui-même comme étant lui aussi un enfant de la mère" (70).

Her name is fluctuating and unstable: she is "la mère" for the children, and Natacha, Emilia, or Hanka Lissovskaïa for the father who desperately tries to enter her reality. She is, we are told very early in the story, a foreigner, literally an exile. She comes from a country whose name remains silent: "Personne, dans son entourage ni dans Vitry, ne savait d'où venait la mère, de quel côté de l'Europe, ni de quelle race elle était" (45). What characterizes her is the absence of origin. She is asleep "dans une sorte de nuit" without language: "Elle disait rien, la mère, voilà, c'était simple, rien, sur rien, jamais" (46).

The lost country is the outside configuration of an inner lost space which tries to express itself in different forms. Of the mother's past only memory traces remain: "Pendant des années la mère s'était souvenue du nom des villages. Maintenant elle les avait oubliés. Elle se souvenait de la couleur bleu du lac Baikal dans l'immensité de neige" (47). The same disappearance of words is manifested in the traces left by the mother tongue:

> La mère a oublié la langue de sa jeunesse [. . .]. Il lui reste de son passé des consonnes irrémédiables, des mots qu'elle paraît dérouler, très doux, des sortes de chants qui humectent l'intérieur de la voix, et qui font que les mots sortent de son corps sans qu'elle s'en aperçoive quelquefois, comme si elle était visitée par le souvenir d'une langue abandonnée. (27)

The past exists in the memory traces left by a tongue long abandoned, a sensuous memory. Of these traces, the most significant is "La Neva," the Russian lullaby, the song without words: "La mère chantait 'La Neva' [. . .]. Sans parole aucune, cette voix racontait le vaste et lent récit d'un amour, de l'amour des amants et aussi la splendeur du corps de leur enfant [. . .] " (111). Her story becomes "embodied" in "La Neva" which links the lost country, the abandoned love and the forgotten mother tongue. For her children she *is* "La Neva." Maternal metaphorical space par excellence, the song occupies the Kristevan semiotic space of the *chora* (a term Kristeva borrows from Plato's *Timaeus*), a "receptacle," a "womb." What characterizes the semiotic space is that it is a "a *pre-signifying* energy" (Grosz, *Sexual Perversions* 42). It belongs to a pre-oedipal stage anterior to the Lacanian mirror-stage which provides the infant with an imaginary, provisional identity. It refers to the order of subject formation, and is composed of anarchic

73

energies (without object or form) which predate the splitting of subject and object. The semiotic is occupied by the indistinguishable presence of mother and child and precedes any linguistic acquisition. The semiotic text is the text of the mother and the text of the child. It lies beyond any narrative utterance. In "La Neva," mother and child occupy the same symbiotic space.[3] The chora, which is "anterior to naming, to the one, to the father and consequently maternally connoted" (Kristeva, qtd. in Grosz 44) is a space of indistinction between same and other. The absent words of "La Neva" will sing this celebration of the indistinguishable bodies of the mother-lover-child. What has been erased, but still lives in traces, is a primary event without signifier. The mother has no origin, she has no tongue. The mother language is a ghost which speaks the original story afraid to be told, the haunting story.

The entrance into exile sanctions for the mother an entrance into abandonment, into oblivion, through an erasure of the original word. The text thus created is woven within her out of a silence which becomes a nurturing, necessary space where haunting images can be regained: "La mère fomentait en elle une œuvre de chaque jour, d'une importance inexprimable, c'était pourquoi elle avait besoin de s'entourer de silence et de paix" (49). The text to be regained is the text of a love twice lived, and twice lost on a night train trav-

---

[3] The words of the actual Russian lullaby may be translated as follows:

May there always be sunshine,
May there always be blue skies,
May there always be mama,
May there always be I.

ersing Siberia. It has its origins in a conversation overheard which spoke of happiness, of a happiness which could not find words, which could be expressed only through signs that pointed toward an absence:

L'homme jeune ne savait pas raconter ça, le bonheur qu'il vivait avec sa femme et ses deux enfants [. . .]. L'homme moins jeune [. . .] lui aussi avait des enfants. Et lui aussi avait parlé du silence de la nuit polaire, de cette conjonction du silence et du froid [. . .]. Le plus jeune avait parlé de l'étrange bonheur des enfants dans ce pays de traineaux et de chiens. (47)

The traces left by that love are those of "une brûlure au cœur" at the core (*corps*) of the mother's being. She has incorporated the story of the two men, and the love for the lost lover, now "massacré par l'oubli," has come to be part of her body, part of her self. Like the other characters who are a projection of her, the mother suffers from that melancholia which (like mourning, Freud reminds us) is a reaction to the loss of a loved object. But "melancholia is in some way related to an object-loss which is withdrawn from consciousness" ("Mourning and Melancholia," Strachey 245). One cannot name the loss, the object is not perceived as object, for "an *identification* of the ego with the abandoned object" has taken place (ibid. 249). The melancholic subject can see the loss of the object but cannot give up the love. In order to preserve that love, the subject incorporates it, for by "taking flight into the ego love escapes extinction" (ibid. 257). The ego is split, the lost object is no longer other, what you have lost is you: "an object-loss" has been transformed into "an ego-loss" (ibid. 249).

The subject is in a state of ambivalence toward the lost object. A love-hate relationship establishes itself, in which the one seeks to maintain the attachment of the libido to the object while the other tries to detach it from the object. The conflict arises in "the region of the memory traces of *things*" (ibid. 256) where words do not exist to express it. One cannot name the loss. The object has to be killed, "massacré," in an attempt to eradicate it, to eradicate the loss.

The melancholic subject who lives in a state of ambivalence lives also in anxieties, in the fear of being abandoned. Every love relationship repeats the loss in a dramatic way. The subject oscillates between being abandoned and abandoning, two terrifying positions, since in each case what is at stake is always the ego. The "fear of losing the object" is also a fear "of losing oneself as object" (Freud, qtd. in *Black Sun* 25).

In the case of the mother in *La Pluie d'été*, what has apparently been lost is a stranger loved one night on a train. A stranger without a name, loved without words. From the start his dimension outside language is going to facilitate the incorporation. The scene of love and abandonment is re-enacted throughout the text with different characters who become an expression of the loss: with the father who has for the mother an "inaltérable désir" (76) and lives in the fear that one day "elle disparaisse pour toujours" (74), with the children, for whom "la mort c'était ne plus voir les parents," and whose terror is that "ces parents qu'ils avaient jamais plus ils ne les reverraient" (52). Ernesto and Jeanne, in their love "savent dans le silence [. . .] qu'ils vont ensemble vers un événement qui semble encore lointain mais déjà inévitable. Une sorte de fin, de mort. Que peut-être ils ne partageront pas" (103). The mother herself, the one who abandons, lives in the terror of Ernesto leaving her: "Elle dit qu'Ernesto un jour ou l'autre il va nous quitter.

Elle, elle dit qu'elle préfère mourir" (89). Every character is rooted in an emptiness, a space of love delineated by abandonment, by endless replay of the unnamable, original loss.

The quest of the mother is "an ever nostalgic quest for the same as other, for the other as same, within the array of narcissistic mirage [. . .]" (*Black Sun* 248). She will re-enact the loss through incorporating Ernesto and Jeanne, the lovers/children. She knows their story, because it is her own. Made "à l'image de ces deux enfants-là," she knows that "Jeanne c'est elle, la mère." The identification is so complete that they will consummate their love the day after the mother "avai[t] raconté le train de Sibérie avec ce voyageur [. . .] c'était la nuit après [. . .]" (129).

The Father

The father is introduced in the first line of the story: "Les livres, le père les trouvait dans les trains de banlieue" (9). He is directly associated with books by textual contiguity and is in a metonymic relationship with the written word. He is also very early in the work connected to the mother and her silence. They form a unit, "le père et la mère," and a knot, "les parents." From the beginning, the symbolic is in the position of being subverted.

The parents go downtown together to get drunk and to read books. A foreigner from an unnamed country, the father is "Emilio" for the mother, "the father" for the children. He exists in relation to her or to them. His past is hers, he exists only when she enters his life, he has no hi-story. He incorporates her past as his.

77

The link he has with the mother is one of despair (53). He loves her desperately at the place he lost her, on this night train through Siberia, where she left him before she knew him and where he goes back endlessly, borrowing the story, making it his own. He wants to be in the place of her loss, to be that empty space within her, to enter her silence, to translate "cette antériorité si obscure, intraduisible, dont elle avait toujours ignoré qu'un jour elle serait cause d'une si grande souffrance" (61). Out of passion for the mother, he will merge with her lost love, entering an emptiness, a lost space, losing himself in the process. His story is the story of love and loss: her love, her loss.

Little by little, the father will "leave" the mother, and be "abandoned" by her, when Ernesto enters her silence by entering the silent core of the book. From language, the father moves into silence and tries to reintegrate a maternal space which in *La Pluie d'été* (as in other texts, e.g., *Le Vice-consul*) speaks of love and abandonment. In a desperate attempt to enter her love, he enters the space of the children, first by speaking of himself as her child, then by joining the children in the *appentis*, where he participates in their terror of being abandoned: "[L]e père vivait dans l'épouvante de perdre cette femme" (76). She tells him, and he believes her, that one day she will leave and disappear (74, 76). To lose her is for him to lose himself, and she knows it: "[L]a mère éprouvait la même peur pour le père—que sans elle il se perde—" (74). By entering the *appentis* and the abandonment of the children, he penetrates deeper into the loss. He is the twice exiled: exiled by her, and a participant in her exile. When she sings "la berceuse russe" without words, "le père repren[d] le chant en faux russe." Her forgotten tongue becomes his as he invents (finds) it.

His closest relationship to the mother is through their nightly drunken expeditions downtown where they find books in which they read their own story. The books found on the trains and, by extension, the other book found, "le livre brûlé" (12), are from the start ambivalent. They pertain, at the same time, to the realms of the father (he finds them, their language is written), and of the mother (they are found on trains, in the maternal space of the *appentis*, are rooted in silence). They tell and they don't tell.

When the departure of Ernesto and Jeanne sanctions the end of the story read (told) by the characters, the father and the mother will both die entering the silent story (152).

The Children/The Bisexual Womb

The "brothers and sisters" form an indistinguishable body until the last pages of the text. They are apart from the other children: Ernesto and Jeanne constitute a unit, a nucleus similar to the knot of "le père et la mère." Like Ernesto, all the children are closely connected to spaces; they are either part of them, and in a way define them, or are excluded from them. Spaces, in *La Pluie d'été*, delineate exile and alienation; they are also metaphorical spaces of love. Their outer configuration traces an inner womblike structure. They are closed or enclosed (the kitchen, the school, and the garden fall into that category) or, on the contrary, are "toujours ouvert[s]" like the *appentis* or the metaphorical spaces of "La Neva" and "le livre brûlé." Their feminine structure encompasses a masculine function. Spaces, in *La Pluie d'été*, are bisexual.

The first enclosed space mentioned is the garden containing a lonely tree. "Entouré d'une clôture," it is a sterile womb: "Rien n'y poussait" (14). Nothing grows there because of the nameless, solitary tree: a phallic mother rooted in silence. The burned book and the tree will be intertwined in the head and body of Ernesto: "Il avait pensé aux deux choses ensemble, à comment faire leur sort se toucher, se fondre et s'emmêler dans sa tête et dans son corps à lui, Ernesto, jusqu'à celui-ci aborder dans l'inconnu du tout de la vie" (15). The empty garden and its tree, "trait sur une page nue," are an inverted image of the "livre brûlé" whose center is a hole. It is only through Ernesto's reading of the lack in the center of the book that the 'phallic' will acquire a symbolic function. The tree will enunciate the lack.

The other space from which meaning is absent is the school, a masculine space of language where silence has been obliterated by words. It is for Ernesto the space of exile. He refuses to go to school because, he explains, "à l'école on m'apprend des choses que je ne sais pas" (29). Ernesto's rapport with knowledge is ontological. In his world, 'knowing' is intrinsic to 'being'. In school, the "I" is denied access to knowledge. "Je" is defined as the non-knower: "Je ne sais pas." The subject is thus robbed of its being. From knowing subject he passes on to non-knower, a passive object. School is the place of binary oppositions, hence, for Ernesto, the location of exclusion, of alienation. What he experiences there is an ego-split. When he says: "Je ne sais pas," he becomes the empty core which cannot be named; silence becomes a trap.

The house, "la casa," and its nucleus, the kitchen, place of the mother, are temporary locations of exile. The choice of a foreign word implies a feeling of displacement. The house is not "named" in a way. The family does not really "belong" there, is displaced within the house. The kitchen is the mother's space par excellence; it is also an exclusive space. The children, except for Jeanne and Ernesto (who are often identified with the mother), are denied its access, can enter it only when expressly invited (71). This exclusion signals the separation from the maternal body and introduces a break in the signifying chain. In the maternal space of the kitchen, meaning is disrupted. It is the site of disconnected dialogue, an irrational discourse whose meaning lies in the silence behind its utterance. It is the place where the "other of language" expresses itself. The kitchen thus represents, in *La Pluie d'été*, a Kristevan semiotic space. "Semiotic" in the sense that it shows a "pattern or play of forces" within language, "a sort of residue of the pre-Oedipal phase" (Eagleton 189). It is the space of laughter shared by mother and child: "Puis les deux, tout à coup, ils rient. . . oh la la. Ils rient. Ils épluchent, ils rient" (23). Laughter is of the chora, it is an instance of "semiotic impulses harnassed in vocalisation," and corresponds to an infiltration of the symbolic in the semiotic (Grosz 44).[4] The nucleus Ernesto/Jeanne, and its mirror image mother/Ernesto, are part of the semiotic chora, and as such have direct access to its spatial configuration: the kitchen. They

---

4 *La Neva*, this other maternal semiotic space, is also punctuated by laughter.

express the bisexual dimension of the semiotic where sexual divisions do not exist.

If the kitchen is the space of the mother, the *appentis* is the space which belongs to the children. It is located outside the house, in another building. It is described as "une galerie," a passage in a basement. A link between two spaces, two worlds, it is "toujours ouvert pour ces enfants-là et où ceux-ci allaient se réfugier chaque jour [. . .]" (13). Its dimension of enclosed and open space of refuge makes it a maternal space. The mother, though, never goes there. She is indirectly present because, as we are told, the children resemble her, and because of Jeanne who "is" the mother. In the *appentis*, the mother represents the place of alterity. She is there as "image," as "other."[5]

A place of refuge, the *appentis* also *is* the space of abandonment: "[P]resque toujours, ils étaient à l'appentis à cause du froid, du vent, de la peur [. . .]. Cet espace de l'appentis était celui de l'abandon" (75). The children experience abandonment in different ways. For them, to be abandoned means to be loved, but also to be threatened by death. They understand and accept that, in a way, the mother has abandoned them: "Sans comprendre l'abandon, ils le comprenaient" (73). Abandonment is a letting go, "un mouvement d'ouvrir les mains et de lâcher" (73), and an utterance of love: "[I]ls aimaient la mère. Ils aimaient être abandonnés par la mère" (74). Each time the parents go downtown to get drunk, the children live an impending death: "Pour les enfants, la

---

[5] "The dependence on the mother is severed and transformed into a symbolic relation to an other" (Grosz 102).

mort c'était de ne plus voir les parents. Leur peur de mourir en passait par là, ne jamais plus les revoir" (52). Their survival and their identity lie in the nucleus they form as "brothers and sisters," "corps unique [. . .] grande machine à manger et à dormir, à crier, à courir, à pleurer, à aimer" (44). The father shares their space: "Dans l'appentis aussi il va se réfugier pour pleurer" (91). He blames himself for abandoning his children, for not loving them enough "à cause de cette femme, leur mère, [. . .] qui avait pris pour elle tout l'amour dont il était capable" (75).

Locus of abandonment within love, the *appentis* is the space of the unnamable. It is the space of the cry, the language of the loss without words: "Les brothers et les sisters, eux, pleurent de plus en plus souvent, mais tout bas [. . .] ils ne disent jamais rien sur les causes de cet empêchement à vivre qui les menace" (104).

Semiotic space of silence, of the unspeakable, the *appentis* is also the space where naming can and does occur. The position of "other" occupied by the mother in the *appentis* allows the symbolic to infiltrate it. In the *appentis*, Ernesto tells the teacher about the first words he wrote. They were for his sister: "J'écrivais que je l'aimais," he confesses. In the *appentis* words can and do name love. Here the "instituteur" teaches the children how to read and write. Upon entering the symbolic order they will acquire a name (113), a personal identity. In the *appentis*, the "livre brûlé" is found, and the story comes into being out of silence. With the discovery of the book, the *appentis* becomes a creative womb which subverts the symbolic. When the father and the "instituteur" go there, they enter the "other of language," a space within language which speaks of love and silence. In the *appentis*, words become the expression of an inner emptiness, they are the signs of a gap. This "emptiness that is intrinsic to the beginnings of the symbolic function appears as the first separation between what is not yet an *Ego* and what is not yet an *object*" (Kristeva, *Tales of Love* 24).

If the maternal space of the kitchen delineates a semiotic chora, the *appentis* illustrates a passage between two realms, between two orders which inflect and penetrate each other. It seems to represent a thetic phase, which, says Kristeva, "marks a threshold between two heterogeneous realms: the semiotic and the symbolic" (*The Kristeva Reader* 102). It is the precondition for the positing of language, and is marked by an influx of the semiotic which disturbs the symbolic, remodels it. The thetic institutes a break between the signifier and the signified. In the *appentis*, the semiotic chora funtions within the signifying device of language. And silence speaks.

The words of the *appentis* are written in the absent core of Ernesto's "livre brûlé" where they tell a story of love and abandonment, the story of the exiled ego.

The Child-King: *Le Pays venant*

> J'entendais les cris, les bruits de la récréation.
> Je crois que j'ai eu peur.
> Je ne sais pas de quoi [. . .]
> Je suis sorti de la classe [. . .]
> J'ai marché très lentement [. . .]
> La peur avait disparu [. . .]
> Je crois que j'ai dormi [. . .]
> Silence.
> Ernesto oublie, dirait-on.
> Et puis il se souvient. (35)

The poem told by Ernesto to explain his leaving school delineates a journey, a path from language to silence through terror and darkness. It is the passage from a pronoun subject, "je" (without memory, without knowledge), to a subject who has a name and remembers. The end of the journey is the remembrance and the dawn of a new language.

Ernesto, we are told, can read and write without having been taught. When he leaves the school, he subverts the order of the symbolic. The order of language, where reigns the law of the father, "is 'erected' only on the basis of repression of the maternal" (Grosz 49). The silencing of the semiotic feminine chora is the necessary condition for the establishment of the coherent text of the symbolic. It is the precondition of patriarchal knowledge. When Ernesto tells how he left school, he establishes himself as an enunciative subject: "[I]l parle très lentement, son discours est apparemment très clair" (34). But what he tells is of the body, of the maternal semiotic order of anarchic feelings, rhythms, movements, sensations, which exist before and beyond the naming. It is this subversive position which allows Ernesto to enter silence, to forget (to enter oblivion, to obliterate), and through the erasure, to remember. He is at the center of *La Pluie d'été*, introduced in the text with the discovery of "le livre brûlé": "Dans les jours qui avaient suivi la découverte du livre brûlé Ernesto était entré dans une phase de silence" (13). At that precise moment of discovery, he leaves the order of the symbolic.

Right from the start, the "livre brûlé" is defined by silence. It signifies not because of its symbolic function as a written text, but because of its lack: its center is silent, burnt. It appears to have been violently emptied of its core by "on ne savait pas quel engin

85

mais qui devait être d'une puissance terrifiante, genre chalumeau ou barre de fer rougie au feu" (13). Words which once were there have been lost, obliterated, through a terrifying violence. The mother-text has been raped. The symbolic function of the phallus stands silent in the garden. Terror and silence have replaced language. The burned book tells the name of Oedipus and the silence of Jocasta.

Ernesto enters the "trou [. . .] parfaitement rond" (13) at the core of the "livre brûlé." He enters silence and finds, invents the story that does not want to be told. The text of the burned book is the text of *La Pluie d'été*, the text of the mother: read, invented by the son. The story he reads, the story he tells: of the Jewish king, of his parents ("les derniers rois d'Israël"), and his own. The text of the burned book is the text within.

The silent core tells the silent story of the unspeakable, and signals the irretrievable loss. Only Ernesto, because he enters the loss, can name it. To find the words, to name silence, is to name the unrepresentable. At the core of the book he reaches "l'inconnu du tout de la vie." At the core of silence, he understands that "la connaissance change[ait] de visage" (109). What the incestuous lovers in the "région silencieuse" knew they shared was the inevitable death awaiting them, which embraced a new knowledge, a luminous knowledge deciphered in the silence of the words:

> Dès lors qu'on est entré dans cette sorte de lumière du livre on vit dans l'éblouissement [. . .]. Ici les mots ne changent pas de forme mais de sens [. . .] de fonction [. . .]. Vous voyez, ils n'ont plus de sens à eux, ils renvoient à d'autres mots qu'on ne connaît pas, qu'on n'a jamais lus ni entendus [. . .] dont on n'a jamais vu la forme mais dont

on ressent [. . .] la place vide en soi [. . .] ou dans l'univers
[. . .]. (109)

The words become the expression of an inner
emptiness, the sign of a gap. Born of an unknown,
unrepresentable darkness, their referent is nothing.

The silent words of "le livre brûlé" transport
Ernesto into the "jamais," outside of chronological
time, that is, outside of the symbolic order. He
evolves in what Kristeva calls the "unspoken of the
spoken," the "truth" which has "neither a before nor
an after [. . .] refuses, displaces and breaks the symbolic order before it can re-establish itself." By recognizing the unspoken in the words of "le livre brûlé,"
Ernesto enters the "truth" which "can be imagined
only as a woman" (*The Kristeva Reader* 153).

In order to recognize (*re-connaître*), one must first
know (*connaître*). Ernesto recognizes the language of
the burned book because he already knew it. When
he invents the words, reads the story, he enters the
metaphor which, says Kristeva, "should be understood as movement toward the discernible, a journey
toward the visible" (*Tales of Love* 30).

Ernesto re-enters the semiotic maternal chora when
he leaves school. He exists simultaneously in the pre-
oedipal world of the imaginary and in the world of the
symbolic. By entering the gap of silence, by inventing
the words, "recognizing the unspoken in all
discourse," that is, by summoning this "truth" which
gives back its meaning to the text, he learns to read in
the story of his "pre-history," which is the absent
story.

When Ernesto learns that "la lecture c'était une
espèce de déroulement continu dans son propre corps
d'une histoire par soi inventée" (16), he understands

that reading demands an incorporation. In the reading of the burned book the object which is incorporated is a silent speech. The metaphorical other with whom Ernesto identifies is silence. "When the object that I incorporate is the speech of the other—precisely a non-object, a pattern, a model—I bind myself to him in a primary fusion, communion, unification. An identification," Kristeva comments (*Tales of Love* 26).

The identification with silence is an identification with that "impossible love never reached, always elsewhere, such as the promises of nothingness, of death" (*Black Sun* 13). The burned book and its emptiness become a metaphor for the unnamable, unrepresentable *Thing*, that "Autre absolu du sujet" (Lacan, *L'Ethique* 65) which "no word could signify" (*Black Sun* 13), and whose form is this "place vide en soi ou dans l'univers." The *Thing* which for Freud reveals itself as a cry, is found by Lacan in the "mot": "[M]ot [. . .] c'est ce qui se tait." The *Thing* (or *rien*) shows up in that which is silent (*L'Ethique* 68).

Kristeva sees in the primary identification with the Freudian father in individual pre-history the possible "means, the link that might enable one to become reconciled with the loss of the Thing" (*Black Sun* 13). What is appealing in this theory is that the "Imaginary Father" located in the pre-oedipal phase is "the same as both parents," since "there is no awareness of sexual difference during that period [. . .]" (*Tales of Love* 26). The Imaginary Father functions as a "bridge between the maternal chora and the symbolic father" (Grosz 88), structuring the space where language expresses, in a satisfactory way, the anarchic impulses and energies of the semiotic. In this space of reconciliation where there is no rupture, no division, the *pays perdu* is also the *pays venant*.

V

BATTAMBANG: THE UNNAMABLE

Robin Lydenberg

In her book *Black Sun: Depression and Melancholia*, Julia Kristeva demonstrates that any effort to account for the unnamable in the language of reason is ultimately reduced to a hopeless tautology: the unnamable is that which is unnamable, "the Thing. Nothing [. . .] the unsignifiable [. . .] death" (53).[1] In our contemporary collective grief, or in the individual experience of melancholia, this unnamable "Thing" carries the ultimate value. As the empty center of psychic life, it constitutes what Kristeva describes as "a black hole—like invisible, crushing, cosmic antimatter" (*BS* 87). In the state of melancholia, the symbolic language of representation and logic becomes dysfunctional, ruptures into discontinuities, gaps and silences. But these breaks are also breakthroughs which release other energies kept in check by the symbolic order—the energies of the semiotic chora: rhythms, alliterations, polyvalence, even nonsense. These semiotic modes may give expression to the unnamable in a new language, or more accurately in a return to an old presymbolic maternal language which has the force of the uncanny—of something long

---

[1] Further references to this work will appear in the text as *BS*.

89

familiar, but forgotten and estranged. As Kristeva puts it, Duras' novels narrate to the reader's unconscious a mysterious story which is "incomprehensible in a familiar fashion" (*BS* 250).

Duras portrays uncanny characters like the heroine of *Le Ravissement de Lol V. Stein*, who is for the narrator of that novel simultaneously unfamiliar and familiar, "gouffre et sœur" (*Lol* 166), but also dramatizes the uncanniness of writing itself. In *Emily L.*, the woman narrator describes her writing as impelled by a memory foreign and isolating, a memory she cannot get over. She writes about things which seem at once necessary ("J'aurais dû m'y tenir toute ma vie") and forbidden ("J'aurai dû les passer sous silence," *Emily L.* 48). Writing is thus bound up with what "ought to have remained [. . .] secret and hidden but has come to light."[2] Freud finds the uncanny lurking in doubles, death, repetition and the mother's genitals, the very same sites in which Kristeva recognizes the mute presence of the unnamable. As Hélène Cixous has pointed out, however, Freud also found the uncanny in fiction itself.[3] It is here that both the uncanny and the unnamable find expression and defy explanation.

Kristeva suggests that the work of a writer like Marguerite Duras can operate as an antidepressant, a suggestion in which she counters the condemnation of language as a virus or parasitic disease with the celebration of language as a therapeutic tool. But it is not a question here of choice—language as poison

---

[2] Friedrich Schelling quoted by Sigmund Freud in "The Uncanny" 224.

[3] Hélène Cixous, "Fiction and Its Phantoms: A Reading of Freud's 'Das Unheimliche'" 546-48.

or language as cure—but of Derrida's "pharmakon": writing as both poison and cure, death and survival.[4] For Kristeva, this hybrid nature of writing comes from its coupling of the symbolic with the semiotic, of a symbolic language recognized and accepted as empty and artificial (an "alien linguistic armor"), with a melancholy affect which only speaks in music, rhythm, alliteration, disconnection, gesture. She calls the result of this coupling a "hypersign" woven "around and with the depressive void [. . .] allegory [in which] I am able to remake nothingness [. . .] within an unchanging harmony [. . .) for the sake of someone else" (BS 99). The language of the hypersign, as it is found in the work of Marguerite Duras, does not function as definition, naming, or the betrayal of the unnamable secret, but is, in Lacan's words, the celebration of "the taciturn wedding of an empty life with an indescribable object."[5] Taciturn, empty, and indescribable, Duras' hypersign is never finalized but always open to translation.

Her novels bear witness to the crushing weight of the unnamable but also to its sublimations—even though they may be partial, temporary and deluded. The reader encounters, sometimes in the background, sometimes dominating the very forefront of Duras' narratives, a collective public consciousness which attempts to domesticate the threatening tensions of the unnamable in anecdotes, gossip and clichés. Town rumors about Lol V. Stein grow into legend and speculation in what the narrator recognizes as the "middle

4   Jacques Derrida, "Plato's Pharmacy" 97-8.

5   Jacques Lacan, "Homage to Marguerite Duras, on Le Ravissement de Lol V. Stein" 129.

class" solution to the unknown. Because the town "n'était pas assez grande pour se taire et avaler l'aventure" (*Lol* 30), it reduced Lol's adventure to the common knowledge of gossip. And so the unnamable is recast in the form of banal chatter or depersonalized newspaper reports. Similarly in *Le Vice-consul* the narrative is punctuated by anonymous fragments of social discourse in which many things are said about the Vice-consul of Lahore, but everyone remains frustrated by the inadequacy of "le dossier," hungry for and expectant of a totalizing account which would contain and neutralize his unspeakable history.

As Maria DiBattista has pointed out, Duras evokes conventional wisdom only to revoke it, and in her narratives the public collective voice (the impersonal "on dit") is always overwhelmed by the force of the unnamable which eludes it.[6] Even in the midst of the most banal social chatter in such settings as Lol's dinner party or the dance in *Le Vice-consul*, some disconnection, some gap will mark its unseemly emergence. Often trivial comments will inadvertently touch the nerve of the unnamable. One voice expresses exasperated irritation at the Vice-consul's inexplicable behavior, "Avec quels mots le dire?" (*VC* 96), while another asks with blasé nonchalance, "Vous ne trouvez pas qu'il est un peu mort?" (ibid. 100). Such remarks seem to say, perhaps, more than they know. The rhetoric of those in command of gossip and conventional wisdom—a rhetoric punctuated throughout with knowing asides ("On dit: Tiens, le voilà [. . .] vous ne savez pas?" 137)—seems like an attempt to hurry past a dizzying abyss keeping eyes

---

6 "The Clandestine Fictions of Marguerite Duras" 284.

firmly fixed on solid ground, never risking the look that might induce an incurable vertigo. Some, like Lol, seem able to exist on several levels at the same time; at her dinner party she talks without listening, focusing on something the others cannot hear (*Lol* 95).

At a level clearly more engaged, more astute than that of gossip or small talk, characters like Jacques Hold and Tatiana Karl come closer to the abyss, witness for a moment the collapse of identity and reality. Jacques Hold seems to accept the limits of knowledge and language, and to proceed, nevertheless, to approximate or even to invent Lol's untellable story. Susan Suleiman has argued convincingly that Hold risks a greater entanglement with Lol than Freud was willing to take on with Dora, or Breton with Nadja ("Nadja, Dora, Lol V. Stein [. . .]" 142-43), yet somehow holds himself in check. If he has looked into the crypt which is Lol's unnamable happiness and unhappiness, Jacques Hold is determined to drag that secret out into the light, to fill in the gaps in her history. In *Le Vice-consul*, Peter Morgan wants to perform the same archeological reconstruction on the unthinkable history of the mad beggarwoman from Battambang (*VC* 182). He assures his friends that he will not follow the beggarwoman into her madness, but at the same time he warns them, "j'ai quand même besoin de connaître cette folie" (ibid. 183). Like Jacques Hold, Peter Morgan will resist total abandonment to insure his own survival.

In several interviews, Duras herself would seem to be making a distinction between the male writer—who begins from a pre-established platform or structure, whose encounter with darkness invariably leads to exhumation, clarification, explanation—and the woman writer who translates the darkness without clarifying it, who accepts the unknowable, the unnamable, death.[7] As the woman in *La Maladie de la mort* explains, "Je ne voudrais rien savoir de la façon dont vous vous savez, avec cette certitude issue de la mort, cette monotonie irrémédiable, [. . .] avec cette fonction mortelle du manque d'aimer" (*Maladie* 50). Love comes, she explains, "d'une faille soudaine dans la logique de l'univers [. . .] d'une erreur [. . .]. De tout, d'un vol d'oiseau de nuit, d'un sommeil, d'un rêve de sommeil, [. . .] de soi-même, soudain sans savoir comment" (ibid. 52). The woman writer in *Emily L.* argues that writing is made of just this sort of "sans savoir," of not knowing what you are doing. If writing alleviates her primordial fear, it does so only when she lets it take possession of her life, when she accepts the fact that confronted with the blinding force of something unknowable and unnamable staring you in the face, you will inevitably lie.

However, it is the word not as lie but as truth which continues to seduce Duras' characters, the lure of the word or name that would be the condensation of all mysteries and all stories leading to the promised land of an ideal language. For the people of S. Tahla and even for Jacques Hold, the name Lol Stein contains the whole of her story, as they have already distilled and packaged it. As Tatiana puts it, "Cette crise et Lol ne faisaient qu'un depuis toujours" (*Lol* 13). Yet Lol eludes them all in different ways: in the variations on her name (Lol, Lola, Lol V. Stein, Lola Valérie Stein), in the specter of T. Beach populated for Jacques Hold by twenty women named Lol Stein, in

---

[7] See, for example, Susan Husserl-Kapit, "An Interview with Marguerite Duras" 427-28.

94

the confusion of her naming herself both Lol and Tatiana, in her conviction that she has been "coulée dans une identité de nature indécise qui pourrait se nommer de noms indéfiniment différents, et dont la visibilité dépend d'elle" (ibid. 41).

These instances in which the reassuring equation of name and identity seems to collapse, culminate in the crisis moment in which a "soi-disant Lol Stein" reveals to Jacques Hold the emptiness of all names:

> Qui avait remarqué l'inconsistance de la croyance en cette personne ainsi nommée sinon elle, Lol V. Stein, la soi-disant Lol V. Stein? Fulgurante trouvaille de celui que les autres ont délaissé, qu'ils n'ont pas reconnu, qui ne se voyait pas, inanité partagée par tous les hommes de S. Tahla aussi définissante de moi-même que les parcours de mon sang [. . .]. Pour la première fois mon nom prononcé ne nomme pas [. . .]. Notre dépeuplement grandit. Nous nous répétons nos noms [. . .]. L'éternel Richardson, l'homme de T. Beach, on se mélangera à lui, pêle-mêle tout ça ne va faire qu'un, on ne va plus reconnaître qui de qui, [. . .] on va se perdre de vue, de nom, on va mourir ainsi d'avoir oublié morceu par morceau, temps par temps, nom par nom, la mort. (112-13)

Emptiness, repetition, forgetting, death: this is the itinerary Jacques Hold sees open up before him and from which he will retreat. As Susan Cohen has observed, once divested of his name, Jacques Hold is free to dissolve into shifting pronouns, even into the impersonal and indefinite "on," to merge anonymously with "l'éternel Richardson."[8] In constructing the narrative of Lol's ravishment, however, Hold regains

8 "Phantasm and Narration in Marguerite Duras' *The Ravishing of Lol V. Stein*" 274.

control of himself, makes all paths lead to his presence in her story, "la distance est couverte, moi" (*Lol* 74).

Can we separate Duras as author from the male writers she depicts? Is there a literary sublimation that could be regenerative and creative rather than narcissistically reductive? Traces of such a reading can be found, I think, in the ways Duras points not only to the limits of language, but to something beyond it. There are, for example, those silent scenes in which characters come together without words, meeting only in the rhythm of dancing or the locked gaze, Tatiana and Lol staring into the same void. There are scenes rendered silent because observed across distance or obstruction, scenes in which language is merely overheard in chance scraps and fragments, set free from the controls of logic and propriety. Lol overhears the dancing couple at the Ball murmur, "peut-être qu'elle va mourir" (*Lol* 104); and as the substitute couple passes her gate years later, she catches the phrase, "morte peut-être" (ibid. 38). Death, what remains unspeakable and unrepresentable even to the unconscious, shows itself in these floating signifiers, not anchored by any clearly designated speaker or certain referent.

When Jacques Hold spies on Tatiana and Lol in conversation and cannot hear their words, he imagines a dialogue he reads at the semiotic level of gesture and facial expression. Conversations one cannot quite hear seem to suggest a more subtle because less tangible language, a language which *might* speak the unnamable without distortion, without reduction, without lies. In a more impatient, or perhaps more pessimistic frame of mind, Tatiana hopes only for a lie she might be able to see through—knowing that the truth she seeks would be blinding and fatal if spoken without this detour through conventional language.

When Lol explains the peculiar quality of her voice as the result of her being hard of hearing, one wonders: Is it because she cannot quite hear conventional speech that she overhears another language, the one that speaks the unnamable? Or is it because she hears this more primordial language of sorrow that she is almost deaf to ordinary discourse? Perhaps Lol has heard that single word which makes you deaf to all other words, which renders all other words empty. Lol's silence is her belief in, her expectant waiting for that single word, "un mot-absence, un mot-trou" which would name her shattered self, her non-identity, her happiness and her despair. It is, of course, a non-existent word which waits "au tournant du langage" (*Lol* 48), always just out of reach. It is a word which cannot be uttered, but which can perhaps be made to reverberate, to vibrate on the level of semiotic rhythm. Perhaps this word shows its shadow in the "frénésie monotone" of the two notes John Bedford practices over and over on his violin, the "chant de l'instrument même" (ibid.). This single word might be the unobstructed, undistorted voice of language itself. Lol waits for this word, this word to end all words, in patience and silence; Jacques Hold, on the contrary, is impatient to seize it, to utter "un long mugissement fait de tous mots fondus et revenus au même magma intelligible" (ibid. 130). The only language Lol Stein might understand. The discontinuity and stumbling which signal Hold's intermittent encounter with that deeper register of language are neutralized and domesticated in the orderly narration he finally imposes on Lol's story.

Yet there are single words that are made to vibrate and resonate in mysterious ways in Duras' work—the most memorable of which is perhaps *Battambang*, a word that becomes a peculiar background drone to the banalities of social discourse in *Le Vice-consul*. As the anonymous beggarwoman "chante et parle, elle fait des discours inutiles dans le silence profond" (*VC* 181). Battambang, a word which names a place, a lost childhood, a song, a dream of being rocked to sleep with a full belly on the back of a great beast. We are told of the mad beggarwoman that Battambang "la protégera, elle ne dira rien d'autre que ce mot" (ibid. 62). The last remnant of childhood and memory, the joyful song of Battambang—is it the only vestige of a maternal longing? or is it a maddening delusion, nothing but a meaningless and toneless drumming in the mind?[9]

At once familiar and unfamilar, Battambang has the force of the uncanny, it both attracts and repels. Peter Morgan wants to tell the woman's story, the story of her song, by matching the rhythm of her footsteps: "Elle, ce serait une marche très longue, fragmentée en des centaines d'autres marches toutes animées du même balancement— celui de son pas—elle marcherait, et la phrase avec elle" (*VC* 179-80). Similarly, Jacques Hold imagines Lol following him in the street, "chacun de ses pas s'ajoute en Lol, frappe, frappe juste, au même endroit, le clou de chair" (*Lol* 56). This matching of rhythms—this coming together at the level of the semiotic—is a coupling at once gentle and violent. In *Le Vice-consul*, Charles Rossett im-

---

[9] "Relieved of its referential value, the name becomes mythical; the word becomes a song," writes Glassman (65). Editor's note.

agines Anne-Marie Stretter his willing victim, her face smiling and contorted beneath his hand which strokes at first, but then strikes her with "une précision machinale." Thus she becomes an object for him, "organique, instrumentale" (*VC* 203), an object which he plays much like John Bedford plays his violin. But such control and manipulation are mere bravado. When the unnamable pursues Charles Rossett in the shape of that *other* woman, the beggarwoman of Battambang, he retreats in fear from the madness, the bestiality, the raw hunger and laughter which continue to reverberate in Battambang.

Unlike the male writers she depicts, Duras does not flee from that word, but turns toward its face, tenderly feels its pulse. In the dynamics of creative sublimation, as Kristeva describes it, Duras remakes the unnamable Nothingness of *Battambang* "in unchanging harmony, here and now and forever, for the sake of someone else."

VI

DURAS' "LAUGHING CURE" FOR LACAN'S HYSTERICAL LACK

Julia Balén

> Man is in revolt against his carnal state;
> he sees himself as a fallen god; his curse
> is to be fallen from a bright and ordered
> heaven into the chaotic shadows of his
> mother's womb [. . .]. He would be in-
> evitable like a pure Idea, like the One,
> the ALL, the absolute Spirit; and he
> finds himself shut up in a body of lim-
> ited powers. (Simone de Beauvoir, *The
> Second Sex* 164)

Let's say her writing ravishes me. That it leaves
me languishing. Perhaps in the fullness of the knowledge of my own forgetting.[1] Perhaps in the power of
her forgetfulness. Reading her corpus I face mortal-
ity. By rendering tangible the knowledge that we forget and are forgotten she strips naked that "privileged
symptom [of]. . . human being's mental illness"—the
ego.[2] In this moment I love (is it her?), even as she is

---

[1] Allied, perhaps, to "la mémoire sans souvenir" of Michel Foucault.
On this subject, see Carol Hofmann's recent analysis in *Forgetting
and Marguerite Duras*. Editor's note.

[2] Shoshana Felman in her *Jacques Lacan* 12, quoting from *Le
Séminaire I* 22.

100

already gone from her texts like the child-mother who has only "Battambang" to say for eternity as she abandons her children like droppings in her voyage to the landscape of her own mother, *la mer*.

I am not alone. Jacques Lacan, too, is ravished. Reading *Le Ravissement de Lol V. Stein*, he claims, "Cet art suggère que la ravisseuse est Marguerite Duras, nous les ravis" ("Hommage" 131). Does the prostitute ravish the gigolo?[3] Donning insistently gendered and sexual masks, Duras and Lacan seem to share an aim to thereby unmask the dynamics of heterosexual relations in search of where and how they might happen. In his homage to her, Lacan notes, almost regretfully, that "Marguerite Duras s'avère savoir, sans moi, ce que j'enseigne" (ibid. 133).

While an astonishing number of parallels exists between the works of Duras and Lacan (including: the importance of memory and forgetting; the location of love; the construction of gendered subjectivities, the difficulty, if not impossibility, of heterosexual relations; and the fundamental importance of language

---

3 The ways in which Duras takes up the position of prostitute in her writing has been developed by Martha Noel Evans in her *Masks of Tradition* 123-56. Evans claims that "as Duras uncovers and explores the indecency of female writing, she discloses that indecency as a cover for something else: the hidden whoring of all language." As for Lacan, his style has created something of a furor in a variety of circles which bears witness at least to its tendency toward titillation. In an attempt to sum up the stylistic differences between Freud and Lacan, Elizabeth Grosz claims, "Where Freud maintains a 'dignity' beyond reproach in his formal yet cordial reports of sexual matters, Lacan seems to go out of his way to flirt, mock, seduce and insult. To Freud's role as Talmudic patriarch, Lacan plays the gigolo" (*Jacques Lacan* 14).

itself),[4] I believe that Duras' texts show that she knows something more than the would-be master-teacher, Jacques Lacan.

Since Lacan subscribes to the belief that the artist "paves the way" for the psychoanalyst, let us explore the path traced by Duras beyond Lacan's generous claim (that she knows without him what he teaches) to discover the places and manner in which she "precedes" him. While much of her œuvre before 1980 (beginning with *Moderato cantabile,* and especially the "India Cycle") works to ravish the subject and culminates in the cry to "destroy" of *Détruire dit-elle,* in *La Maladie de la mort,* 1982, Duras explores the territory beyond *ravissement,* creating subjectivities in the preludic conditional tense, re-membering the language of childhood games.[5]

Her text suspends time, like hypnosis, so that the reader might remain conscious while traversing the places where thoughts and nerve endings, mind and body interact indistinguishably. In *ravissement,* she renders the madness of phallogocentric subjectivity tangible and suggests a place beyond the need for mastery which engenders madness. Let's say this is a story of my reading Duras.

---

[4] The intersections of their works have been extensively developed by, among others, Mary Lydon, Trista Selous, Marcelle Marini, and Michèle Montrelay.

[5] See *Le Camion* 89, where she speaks of her preference for the future anterior as the "pre-ludic conditional" of French.

"One doesn't say such things"

On the surface, Marguerite Duras' dramati-poetic novel, *La Maladie de la mort*, tells of a man's discovery of—and struggles with—his malady of death and love (*la mort* and *l'amour*) through his perceived possession and loss of a woman's body. The setting, perhaps Duras' most sparse, essentially consists of the man's bedroom. The reader/spectator's gaze remains within this room, for the most part focused on the body of the woman, except for an occasional glimpse through the room, out onto a porch that overlooks the sea, or to a vague social space to which the text merely alludes. The woman's body rarely leaves the bed. Overtly gendered and sexual, the text plays with the materials of the standard romance and of pornography. Duras strips both forms down to their common denominator: desire, not as romance dresses it, nor as pornography idolizes it, but as the excruciating dynamics of its hegemonic, phallic construction sever the subject of desire from embodiment.

Duras begins by stripping subjectivity of the illusion of individuality and the limiting particularity that names allow. No one in the text is named, leaving the reader to swim in a sea of pronouns that forces the issues of generic reference, gender, and individuality. With the opening phrase, "Vous devriez ne pas la connaître," the reader immediately faces a problem of defining selves. Who speaks? And to whom? It becomes clear before the end of the sentence that the "you" addressed, with his "sexe dressé dans la nuit" (7), sports a penis. This may lead the reader to envision "you" as a masculine character to whom the narrator speaks. But "you" is also a direct address to the reader. The thoughts, feelings, and actions which the narrator describes thus become the reader's as s/he addresses "you."

Yet, in another sense, "you" also refers to the speaker, whose strong identification with "you" expressed through the ability to see and speak (for) "you" leads the reader to assume that the narrator is male, even though the gender is never stated in the story.[6] Seen this way, speaking in the second person becomes self-reflective. In the manner of common parlance (you know when you're speaking and everyone understands you) this use of the second person has the effect of placing responsibility outside the self, onto an implied other, thereby rendering the thoughts, the feelings and/or actions of the individual speaker normative, communal, and/or universal. So, even though the narrator speaks as voyeur, the "you" he addresses can also be read as a generic reference to the narrator in the process of speaking to himself. This reading seems reasonable since throughout most of the text the narrator speaks/reads[7] to the reader/"you" as though privy to "your" every thought and feeling, making it possible to read much of the story as though the narrator were speaking aloud to and of himself.

In its construction of identities through the use of pronouns alone and the language's insistence on gender (coupled with the sexual focus of the content), the text simultaneously fractures the illusion of any

---

[6] In her postscript, Duras suggests a male for the theatrical role (56).

[7] Duras offers staging suggestions at the end of the text in which she asks that the narrator read rather than perform the lines because "rien ne remplace le manque de mémoire du texte, rien, aucun jeu" (59). This seems to further support the view of the narrator's reading as a re-membrance of the unconscious, that which has been forgotten.

generic subject and collapses the individualities that subjectivity supposedly represents, thereby rendering "the Subject's" usually transparent, heterosexually masculinized nature opaque. In whatever manner the reader chooses to identify with the text, the construction of identities within it makes manifest the gendered nature of that choice. For example, the reader marked with the feminine, though accustomed to identifying (at least to some degree) with a masculinized generic subject, is pressed to awareness of the ways in which any identification on her part with either "you" or the narrator requires reading like a man. To do so she must empathize with a sex "qui appelle où se mettre, où se débarrasser des pleurs qui remplissent" (7). Perhaps more radically, the masculine reader finds his usually neutral gender status clearly marked and embodied. As sex is rendered explicitly physical, gender thus embodied marks all subjects, leaving none gender-neutral.

If the reader identifies with either the narrator or "you," the pronouns paradoxically render the text both more personally intimate and more generic than the use of character names could possibly do. Potentially three subjects: the narrator, the reader, and "you" (eventually placed in concert with "them") function virtually in unison in the inscription of desire throughout the text and thereby effectively parody the standard masculinized gaze. The reader perceives the story through the narrator's descriptions as he reports voyeuristically on every thought, word, and deed of "you," through whose senses, particularly the visual, the reader/narrator/"you" will collectively experience "her." While the empowered gaze of white western culture is decidedly masculinized such that the world, as feminine, presents itself to the controlling male gaze, this text effectively places the latter and its subject under scrutiny.

"I don't know"

There are two notable exceptions to the narrator's ability to speak for "you" in which he separates himself from "you," and potentially from the reader. These are the only times he speaks as an "I" in the text as though separate from "you." Both times he claims a lack of knowledge:

> Peut-être prenez-vous à elle un plaisir jusque-là inconnu de vous, je ne sais pas. Je ne sais pas non plus si vous percevez le grondement sourd et lointain de sa jouissance à travers sa respiration, à travers ce râle très doux qui va et vient depuis sa bouche jusqu'à l'air du dehors. Je ne le crois pas. (15)

The switch in reference and focus from "you" to "I" suddenly fractures what has been up to this point a unitary gaze, leaving a gap between the speaking and the embodied subject. The thinking/speaking "I" seems at this moment to function separately from the desiring/embodied "you" while at the same time claiming a knowledge of "her" that "you" seem to lack in spite of what the reader might assume to be "your" greater physical proximity to "her" as "you" are in the physical process of giving "her" pleasure. Through the pronoun switch to "I" the narrator distances himself from the actions of "your" body precisely at the moment of "your" pleasure, changing focus instead directly to "her" (instead of perceiving "her" through "you"). In effect, "your" pleasure becomes that which cannot, or will not, be spoken. Or, in light of what has been up to this point a unitary gaze, at the moment of "your" possible *jouissance*, "I" suddenly maintain ignorance of "you." The second instance of "I" repeats the distancing and the claim of ignorance of "your" thoughts and feelings at the moment of possible *jouissance*. The narrator cannot speak it, or refuses to do so.

Similarly, both immediately before and after the narrator's distancing from and silencing of "your" pleasure, "you" physically attempt to silence "hers."

> Par distraction, vous lui donnez de la jouissance et elle crie.
> Vous lui dites de ne pas crier. Elle dit qu'elle ne criera plus [. . .].
> Elle ouvre les yeux, elle dit: Quel bonheur.
> Vous mettez la main sur sa bouche pour qu'elle se taise, vous lui dites qu'on ne dit pas ces choses-là.
> Elle ferme les yeux.
> Elle dit qu'elle ne le dira plus.
> Elle demande si eux ils en parlent. Vous dites que non.
> Elle demande de quoi ils parlent. Vous dites qu'ils parlent de tout, sauf de cela. (14-16)

"They" mark a further fracturing of masculine subjectivity. If the narrator functions as a disembodied voice (at least within the written text),[8] then "they" function as the abstract Other that allows, if not demands, the illusion of disembodiment. Maintaining control over what is spoken and what is not, "they" impose, in Lacanian terms, a "symbolic order" which institutes subjecthood through gender

---

[8] While it would function differently, the performance of this text, for which Duras suggests that the narrator read the text of/to a man who is never physically present, would perhaps even more powerfully display the disembodied nature of masculine subjectivity by embodying disembodiment.

division marked by symbolic "castration." So while there are moments in the text of an insistent division between "you" and "I," or "you" and "them," the fractured parts of the masculine subject remain collapsed through the mutual imposition of the silencing of *jouissance.* The phallic law of silencing pleasure separates what is spoken from the body, separates "you" from "your" self. In fact, these characters correspond to the Lacanian "Schema L" which outlines the psychical agencies of the decentered subject. "I" play the ego, "you" play the id, "they" play the Other and "she" plays the other (*Écrits* 198). Yet, there are striking differences.

First of all, with "their" implied multiplicity, Duras effectively fractures what is otherwise (certainly in Lacanian theory) monolithically constructed as the Other, "the-name-of-the-father," or God, and places the power of symbolic structuring back in the hands of humans. Secondly, Duras takes that which Lacan attempts to contain within the realm of the psycholinguistic and opens it out into the realm of the social, rendering the symbolic system less closed, more open to social critique. Moreover, contrary to popular images of masculinized subjectivity, certainly within the genres of romance and pornography on which this piece plays, this masculine subject is not empowered: "you" are at the mercy of the conflicting desires that traverse "your" flesh in "your" very denial of "your" own embodiment. While these images in some ways parallel Lacan's description of the subject (through the emphasis on embodiment, with "your" penis weeping at the impossibility of getting back to "your" own body), the text builds tension between the silencing of *jouissance* and "your" desire: "De ce corps vous voudriez partir, vous voudriez revenir vers le corps des autres, le vôtre, revenir vers vous-même" (16-17). By placing the physical sign of the phallus, the penis (and its lack), literally embodied in the foreground, Duras alters its ability to play the part of master signifier and displays the constrictions and limitations, if not deformations, of phallically defined identity, gender and meaning.

Not knowing "où poser votre corps ni vers quel vide aimer" (11), "you" enact a desperate, hysterical search of "her" body. "Your" repeated desire to "get back to yourself" states clearly the fractured nature of "your" existence and suggests something beyond and previous to "your" current state to which "you" feel a need to return, but which remains unnamable, unknowable. "Your" anachronistic desire expresses itself in "your" sense of persecution, "your" suffering, "your" story of lack, the weeping of "your" penis, "your" hysterical symptoms.[9] The reader, through identification with the narrator/"you," remains collapsed into this hysterically fractured subject, unless, of course, s/he is laughing with "her."

In contrast to the hysterical male subject, "she" is the fully "other" of the story whose voice resonates against the narrator/"your" voice. "She" is the body through which "you" search to "tenter connaître ça, vous habituer à ça, à ce corps, à ces seins, à ce parfum, [. . .] à ce danger de mise au monde d'enfants que représente ce corps" (8). So while "you" are overtly masculinized before the end of page one, "she" is just as overtly biologically feminized with breasts and implicit pregnancy, and linguistically

---

9 See, on this point, Catherine Clément's descriptions of the hysteric in *The Newly Born Woman* 3-59.

gendered as an uncollapsable "other," that which, within the text, from the point of view of the masculinized gaze, is both abject and desired.[10]

On this level, reading from the masculinized gaze that the text constructs, "she" functions as an object of desire, the Lacanian *objet a*, developed from the infantile *fort-da* game which Freud outlined as the basis for his controversial death drive. Speculating on the basis of his grandson's play with a wooden reel tied with string, Freud writes:

> What he did was to hold the reel by the string and very skillfully throw it over the edge of his curtained cot, so that it disappeared into it, at the same time uttering his expressive 'o-o-o-o'. He then pulled the reel out of the cot again by the string and hailed its reappearance with a joyful '*da.*' This, then was the complete game—disappearance and return [. . .].
>
> The interpretation of the game then became obvious. It was related to the child's great cultural achievement—the instinctual renunciation (that is, the renunciation of instinctual satisfaction) which he had made in allowing his mother to go away without protesting. He compensated himself for this, as it were, by himself staging the disappearance and return of the objects within his reach.
> (*Beyond the Pleasure Principle* 809)

Similarly, "you" enact all the elements related to this infantile stage of development, but this time within the adult sexual theater. The narrator's claim that for "you" she fills "le monde tout entier" (28) describes the position that Freudian theory claims the mother fills for the child in early infancy, before the theorized

---

10 For an extensive development of the notions of abjection and otherness within a psychoanalytic frame, see Julia Kristeva's *Pouvoirs de l'horreur.*

separation of self and other. In Duras' text at the point of separation, "Il n'y a plus rien dans la chambre que vous seul. Son corps a disparu. La différence entre elle et vous se confirme par son absence soudaine" (54). Through repetitious exiting from, and returning to, the feminized body and its parts, the text hysterically re-enacts the inevitable separation of self from (m)other, illustrated in the *fort-da* game as an explanation of the attempt to take control.

"You weep"

Between this dream of symbiosis and the final separation that the text enacts, "you," like the child playing *fort-da*, vacillate between drawing "her" body to "you" in an effort to create that symbiosis, and pushing "her" body away from "you" in an attempt to take control of a painful reality, "pour retrouver votre différence" (36). "De ce corps vous voudriez partir, vous voudriez revenir vers le corps des autres, le vôtre, revenir vers vous-même" (16-17) in what might be read as an impossible desire to return to the womb. This push-pull takes place on three levels, the first of which is a physical coming and going on the part of "you." Repeatedly: "Vous quittez la chambre [. . .] loin de son odeur" (31), then "vous revenez vers le corps" in an obsessive motion that admits of the pain which "cette différence intégrale, qui vous sépare d'elle" (42) causes "you."

The second level of the push-pull motion appears within the gaze, but here it grows more complex. Not only is there an obsessive choice to look and then not look, but time and again "you look" but "can't see anything." The text enacts the horror and consequent denial of castration. Freud claims that the fear of castration begins when the little boy discovers that Mommy doesn't have one. He cannot see hers. In Duras' text:

> Vous dites: Je ne vois rien [. . .]. Vous prenez le corps, vous regardez ses différents espaces, vous le retournez, vous le retournez encore, vous le regardez, vous le regardez encore.
> Vous abandonnez.
> Vous abandonnez. Vous cessez de toucher le corps.
> Jusqu'à cette nuit-là vous n'aviez pas compris comment on pouvait ignorer ce que voient les yeux, ce que touchent les mains, ce que touche le corps. (22)

Later: "[V]ous allumez des lampes pour la voir. Pour la voir elle. Pour voir ce que vous n'avez jamais connu, le sexe enfoui, voir cela qui engouffre et retient sans apparence de le faire, de le voir ainsi refermé sur son sommeil, dormant" (28-29). "You" can choose to walk away or close "your" eyes because these are actions within "your" control, but to want to see and not be able to see seems to be a symptom of "your" horror at the discovery of difference, the reality of corporality, of difference and separation expressed in the power of the mother to walk away from the child.

Another complexity of the gaze which, according to psychoanalytic theory, develops during the mirror stage, is the concern with who is seeing whom, with where the self ends and the other begins. Thus, there is not only the theorized horror (at least for the child who sports a penis) in realizing that Mommy doesn't have one, but the horror also that, not only can you look at her, but she can see you. In Duras' portrayal of the masculine subject's hysterical re-enactment, "[v]ous découvrez qu'elle vous regarde. / Vous criez"

(25). "Your" panic at realizing "she" is "other" and that "her" gaze functions as "la frontière infranchissable entre elle et vous" (25) marks the beginning of the weeping in the text. "[V]ous pleurez sur vous-même comme un inconnu le ferait . . . [et] ne comprenez pas comment il est possible qu'elle ignore vos pleurs" (27-28). Highlighting the (male) child-centered nature of narratives of desire in a phallic economy, Duras implies a world beyond Lacan's phallically defined universe which naturalizes/ neutralizes this point of view.

Finally, the tension between the push-pull of the *fort-da* is most clearly expressed on the level of pulsions, or drives. On the one hand, for "you," "her" body "appelle [. . .] le déchaînement des passions entières, mortelles" (21). Yet, throughout the text these violent desires find resolution in the weeping of "your" penis as it takes "cette route aveugle" (13) because: "On dit que ça résiste plus encore, que c'est un velours qui résiste plus encore que le vide" (10); and so that "vous ayez moins peur de ne pas savoir où poser votre corps ni vers quel vide aimer" (11); "pour dormir sur le sexe étale, là où vous ne connaissez pas [. . .] pleurer là" (9). Sex under these circumstances may momentarily resolve "your" violent passions, but it does not constitute sexual relations. Moreover, it conflates love and death (*la mort* and *l'amour*). The closing line, "vous avez pu vivre cet amour de la seule façon qui puisse se faire pour vous, en le perdant avant qu'il soit advenu" (57), offers a way to interpret the malady of death and love from which the masculinized subject suffers. Theoretically it describes the bond we have with our mothers, which we lose before the constitution of our cognizant selves. We are severed from our mothers and may interpret the symbiotic bond of infancy as love long after it has been broken, says Kristeva (*Héréthique* 30). This means that the infantile love that "you" search for in "her" body is not possible in the present, but only in reconstructed memory.

The story begins with a conditional phrase, "Vous devriez ne pas la connaître," and slips between the present tense and the conditional throughout. This slippage creates a sense that, as in childhood games, that which is desired is actually happening, with a dream-like realism. Like the child who incorporates the death of a parent into play, this text calls on the sense of safety offered by fiction while traversing the dangerous territory of the psycho-sexual. Under the guise of being only a figment of the masculine subject's imagination, "she" breaks into the symbolic order that would render "her" an object. From this psycho-linguistically structured beyond, "she" speaks.

> [O]ne might be able to interpret the fact of being deprived of a womb as the most intolerable deprivation of man. (Luce Irigaray, *Speculum of the other Woman* 23)

"She laughs"

I suppose that one might read *La Maladie de la mort* without ever moving beyond the gaze of the reader/narrator/"you"/ "them" that it forms—without ever identifying with "her." Objectification of women remains more the norm than the exception in western culture, and the text more or less empathetically follows a male character through infantile desires to reconnect with the mother, restaged in an adult sexual setting (not too strange in a post-Freudian world).

From this vantage point, the masculine world that Duras portrays (for both male and female subjects/ readers) is, like Lacan's, empty, lonely, and repleat with unfulfillable desire. But "her" laughter makes this masculinized reading very difficult, if not inaccurate. Playing in the space shared by mothers and whores, those who offer their bodies to fill the "needs" of others, "she" smiles from beginning to end, like a sphinx, ironically, with knowledge of something beyond the perceptions of the child, beyond the gaze of the text. As all of our first loves were, ostensibly, our mothers, "your" desire is theoretically non-gendered. So, while the surface of the text is overtly gendered, the passion it expresses theoretically is not. The whole of the story might be seen as an enactment of the mirror and Oedipal stages of development, but with a difference.

The description of ejaculation as a penis that must "se débarasser des pleurs qui remplissent" (7) puts a feminized twist on masculine desire and thereby revises the metaphor as old as Oedipus that equates sight with the penis, the one-eyed man. Masculine vision, or the gaze that needs "her" as its object, is blurred by these tears, ironically, in a manner similar to the way in which tears blur the vision of the traditional woman of romance. But the standard masculine hero cannot come forward with a clearer vision, or some gaze constructed as truth/power that might enable him to rescue "you" from distress. Rather, the text effectively undermines the power of any gaze, even its own, to render anyone simply an object in a manner similar to the way the narrator/"your" gaze attempts to objectify "her." The gaze of the text unveils the workings of the masculinized gaze, the masculinization of subjectivity, and the emotional cost of that masculinization: "you" seem condemned to forever miss the present(s)/presence of love due to "your" need for "her" body to establish "your" subjectivity.

In contrast, "she" accepts the paid nights out of curiosity, not out of unfulfillable need. When asked why "she" agreed to the proposal to sleep with the man, "she" answers, "Parce que dès que vous m'avez parlé j'ai vu que vous étiez atteint par la maladie de la mort. Pendant les premiers jours je n'ai pas su nommer cette maladie. Et puis ensuite j'ai pu le faire" (23). In a curious, almost affectionately de-tached manner throughout, "she" seems to study "you" like a prostitute/mother who does not take her role too seriously, who knows herself to be separate from the role she plays for an/other, and pleasures in the difference. "Her" actions seem to be more freely chosen, less fetishizing, differently driven than "yours," even when "she" accepts "your" conditions. "She" also is the one who names "your" malady and offers "her" body, for a time, as a place for "you" to attempt to work out "your" conflation of love and death. Yet "she" clearly lives and loves differently and beyond the realm of the text. "Her" actions and words belie a life beyond "your" limited, infantile, masculinized gaze. There is more to "her" than what the narrator's ("your") gaze offers. "She" exceeds the male subject's ability to see "her" on more than—or even just—the bodily level.

Enacting the violence of gendering that language both naturalizes and requires, the text literally splits the reader between the overtly sexualized bodies of "you" and "her," thereby exaggerating the process of genderization itself to display both its absurdity and its linguistic necessity. Identification of any sort on the part of the reader requires an uncomfortable gender consciousness that foregrounds the inevitable objectification required by language, thereby rendering the generic reference to "the subject" untenable through embodiment. By emphasizing the embodiment of masculinity, not as it hegemonically claims the space of the neutral, but as it presents itself to a subject marked with the feminine; by rendering the phallus physically present as a weeping penis searching through the body of another in hopes of finding itself, the text deconstructs the ability of the masculine subject to function generically.

If the Freudian *desidero* radically alters the ability of the *cogito* to establish existence, then Duras' play with Freud's phallically constructed *desidero* functions in as disconcerting a manner through its parody of the subject of language, the assumed generic self. And while Lacan's psycho-linguistically constructed phallic subjectivity reinscribes a universal (dis-embodied) phallic power at the moment it acts as though to undermine it, Duras re-embodies the male subject so as to leave no gender neutral. In the process the reader/narrator/"you" become Man, not in the grand universal sense that marginalizes all who do not fall under the rubric, but in the same personally limiting, essentialized manner in which Woman limits women to the biological. If "la femme n'existe pas,"[11] then neither does "l'homme."

The malady constructed by the text, a malady of the masculinized, is the real hysteria. It is the illness that fears a wandering womb—one that can no longer be home to the child—that the child, and most cer-

---

[11] As Lacan claims in his controversial *Séminaire XX: Encore.*

tainly the man, cannot control. Duras' text implies that the hysteria Freud found, was his own mirrored in (reflected onto the mirror of) his objectification of the women he diagnosed. The wandering womb troubles masculinized subjects because they construe subjectivity as dependent upon heterosexualized genderization and the maintenance and control of otherness. In Duras' text, upon acknowledging "your" substantial difference, the masculinized subject meets with "your" malady of death and enacts a hysterical search for a womb "you" cannot have. The futility of this search and absurdity of the condition are expressed in "your" lack of presence.

Ravished, Lacan praises the "hopeless charity" with which he believes Duras expresses abundant faith in what he barely dares to name, that is, love. But Lacan (mis)reads her works from the masculinized gaze that her texts critique. It is not abundant faith that Duras shows, but faith in abundance, an abundance for which phallically constructed desire, born of lack, creates an Other. Duras does not romanticize the othering process, the desire for/of the Other; rather, she "laughs" in love. Beyond *ravissement*, let's say that I am laughing with "her."

VII

MEMORY AS ONTOLOGICAL DISRUPTION:
HIROSHIMA MON AMOUR
AS A POSTMODERN WORK

Anne-Marie Gronhovd
William C. VanderWolk

Any categorization of a work of art is problematic, any attempt to call it postmodern so fraught with difficulty as to render the endeavor foolhardy. We approach this analysis of *Hiroshima mon amour* with due caution, but also with the hope that by freeing the work from the constraints of epistemological scrutiny, its true depth may become evident in the play of ontological disruption. Conclusions about plot, character, narration, time, psychology and history will then give way to questions, to an indeterminacy that is postmodern in nature and rich in implication for the reader/spectator. Rather than the story of a woman who finds a kind of salvation through memory and forgetting, *Hiroshima mon amour*, in our view, is many stories, each unresolved. The result is a work whose strength lies in possibility rather than certainty, in the postmodern question of what might have been, in alienation and absence, and in the disruption of expectation.

The first question that arises in discussing *Hiroshima* is which "text" to use. Duras' screenplay contains a synopsis giving information and analysis that the film cannot provide. The film, on the other hand, shows us the power of the flashback, a technique appropriately absent from the screenplay. Critics who seek fixed conclusions have chosen one or the other. This essay proposes a postmodern reading/viewing in which free reign may be accorded the ideas found in the screenplay *and* the film, concentrating on the quintessentially Durassian "text" underlying both.

Clearly, postmodernism cannot be defined, or at least, it resists definition. Always aligned with indeterminacy and silence, it cannot be placed within established limits. It would be easier to identify *Hiroshima* as a product of modernism, "nourished in part by its concern with a relationship between narration and the unconscious on one hand and the ludic play of structure on the other" (Turim, *Flashbacks in Film* 225). These relationships are indisputably present in *Hiroshima*, but other dimensions of the work are better explored in light of the postmodern. Lyotard writes: "[Modern aesthetics] allows the unpresentable to be put forward only as the missing contents; but the form, because of its recognizable consistency, continues to offer to the reader or viewer matter for solace and pleasure [. . .]. The postmodern would be that which, in the modern, puts forward the unrepresentable in presentation itself; that which denies itself the solace of good forms [. . .] that which searches for new presentations" (*The Postmodern Condition* 340). *Hiroshima mon amour* is representative of such a definition, as it seeks, through fragmentation and indeterminacy, its own form.

Form is not, however, the sole consideration. Brian McHale and Dick Higgins see a distinct difference between the types of questions modernists and postmodernists ask: "The dominant of modernist fiction is epistemological [. . .]. 'How can I interpret this world of which I am a part? And what am I in it?' The dominant of postmodern fiction is ontological. [...] 'Which world is this? What is to be done with it? Which of my selves is to do it?'" (Higgins cited by McHale 9, 10). The second set of questions articulates more clearly Duras' project. There exists in *Hiroshima* no ontological grounding from which epistemological questions can take shape. We have only possibilities of who the characters might be and of what kind of world they inhabit. "When you cross from knowledge to a fictional world of what might be (have been) you pass from modernism to postmodernism," writes McHale (10). The difficulty for us as critics is to find a means of expressing possibilities while using language that fits more comfortably into epistemological research. For help we turn to Ihab Hassan.

Hassan sees postmodernism as an historical period (roughly post-World War II); as a set of characteristics, some or all of which apply to postmodern works; and as a way of reading that can be applied to a variety of works. The postwar period in which *Hiroshima* is set saw the questioning of the principles upon which the modern world rests. Like Beckett and the New Novelists, Duras portrays the uncertainty and anxiety of that era, and *Hiroshima mon amour*, in its fragmentation, indeterminacy, subversion, polychronicity, repetition, and silence, may well be "a theoretical description of [that] universe" (Thomas Pavel cited in McHale 27) rather than an epistemological questioning of the characters' role in a world known to us all.

Our thesis relies on the process of remembering and forgetting (*la mémoire et l'oubli*), two elements that are interdependent. Putting her memories into words affords the protagonist of *Hiroshima* a means of forgetting, of working through the pain of memory (*la douleur de la mémoire*). "Dans *Hiroshima*, c'est la douleur de voir la passion passée ne resurgir que pour mourir. La mémoire de l'oubli est la phase longuement et péniblement déterrée par l'héroïne et elle aboutit à l'oubli de la mémoire" (Guers-Villate 99). Memory is impossible without forgetting, a kind of dismembering that operates through transformation, fragmentation, alienation and absence.

"Elle," the protagonist of *Hiroshima*, recognizes the link between memory and forgetting, but no synthesis arises from her experience. *Hiroshima* is not a work of fulfillment through memory, but rather a splitting apart of any possible conjunction of memory, the characters' personal stories, and history (*mémoire, histoire, Histoire*). Fragments of memories, history, language, love, and even the characters' bodies separate, reform, and separate again in a continuous, dizzying movement resulting in a postmodern alienation of the reader/spectator. This, for us, is what gives *Hiroshima mon amour* its force.

Fragmentation

The opening scene of *Hiroshima* can be viewed as a synopsis of all that we could say about the role of fragmentation in the text. Parts of the bodies of the French woman and the Japanese man are seen intertwined but never whole. Once we realize what is being portrayed, we, like the characters themselves, try to reassemble the pieces. "The film's opening sequence produces in us an anxiety and a desire to identify a human body as an unmutilated integrity" (Willis 35), but bodies in the text and in the film always appear as de-membered and can only be reassembled through memory. Like the various pieces of a puzzle scattered in an attempt to reconstruct an image or meaning never realized, the hand of the sleeping Japanese lover and the hand of the dying German soldier in Nevers become interchangeable. Both are contrasted with the gnarled hand of the victim of the bomb at Hiroshima; faces are conspicuously separated from bodies, as in the image of the French girl (in the cellar of her home in Nevers) juxtaposed to the face of a black cat, or the face of the German superimposed on the naked upper bodies of the lovers at Hiroshima. It is this process that allows the creation of the fiction and establishes the tension between the surface (the love story) and meaning (the historical context). "Le fantasme du morcellement du corps, qui a donc à voir avec tous les désirs et ces peurs" (Borgomano, *Duras* 184) opens the text and is present throughout.

Juxtaposed to the characters' fragmented bodies are shots of the victims of the bombing of Hiroshima. This second level of narration enters our consciousness just as it entered the French woman's: through film. She has been to the museum in Hiroshima several times; she has seen the mutilated bodies depicted in cinematic reproductions of the horror. Yet the voice of her Japanese lover has already called into question her ability to see Hiroshima; he has challenged the capacity of reconstruction (filmic memory) to translate real events. "Tu n'as rien vu à Hiroshima" contains his spoken denial of her contention that she has seen everything in Hiroshima, and his use of the conditional, "Sur quoi aurais-tu pleuré?" sheds more doubt on her affirmation. At the same time, the utterance forces us to wonder what *he* has seen at Hiroshima. As he tells her, he was not in the city the day of the bombing. Ironically enough, he was lucky, he was at war:

> Lui
> Ma famille, elle, était à Hiroshima. Je faisais la guerre.
> Elle
> Une chance, quoi? (39)

What remains, then, is the image of what might have happened to him had he been there. We are struck by the inherent impossibility of *anyone* having *seen* what happened at Hiroshima, since even the survivors must have been at least temporarily blinded by the impact of the bomb. In a short opening scene, then, the major themes of the work have been presented: love, memory, history, and the impossibility of closure. Only fragments remain, corporal and historical disconnections that strip all certainty from the characters' and the spectators' experiences and expectations. The fragmented body of text and film has metonymically adopted the anguish of the apocalyptic aspects of the atomic disaster.

Temporal disconnections quickly become evident in *Hiroshima mon amour*. Beyond the second level of narration, the historical, lies a third which exists only in the memory of the young woman. However, her memories of Nevers do not afford her any special understanding of either the past or the present. On the contrary, as they take clearer shape, and as she recounts them to the Japanese man, her experiences, past and present, become *more* fragmented, resulting in a de-membering of her notion of love, experience, and time. Memory ceases to function as an organizing force capable of synthesis and healing. It becomes instead an agent of disjunction, a trait which the cinema is particularly able to portray.

Flashbacks and the kind of "stop-go image presentation" (Willis 47) found in *Hiroshima mon amour* fragment narration itself and blur distinctions between dream and reality as well as between past and present. The constant movement from narrative present to past and from present to future destabilizes the narration to the point of alienating the spectator. The gesture that brings back an event or an image to erase it as soon as it has appeared in the text or on the screen, articulates a desire to avoid an absolute form in fiction. Thus our attention will be captured, our senses put on alert, our memory, both experiential and intertextual, awakened so as to engage us in Duras' postmodern dance of indeterminate content and form.

Indeterminacy

Memory, the servant of forgetting, lies at the heart of all that is indeterminate about Duras' project. Memory inevitably transforms lived experience to the point where a specific memory says as much about what has been forgotten or repressed as about the actual lived experience. In *Hiroshima* Duras shows us through flashbacks to Nevers and Hiroshima that the French woman undergoes what Freud called a "screen memory." What has the French woman seen?

> J'ai tout vu. Tout.
> Non, tu n'as rien vu à Hiroshima. (22-23)

125

Her vision of historical events in Japan comes from films seen in a museum, films that reconstruct history, literal screen memories. Yet she has been profoundly affected by the same war, and, by viewing the films, she is drawn back into her past while keeping a safety screen between her present and her past. Real danger approaches for her only when she begins to recount those lived experiences. She fears the pain of memory as much as she fears the oblivion of history.

If, as Jean Pierrot contends, involuntary memory is for Duras the only way of truly recreating the past (*Marguerite Duras* 107), then moments such as the evocation of the dying German's hand through observation of the sleeping Japanese lover are the only instances of truth in the film. By creating ambivalence on all fronts—narrative, referential, emotional—Duras strips the text of limits, leaving free the interplay of memory, both voluntary and involuntary, among the reader/spectator, the characters, and the text. It matters very little what is true. What might be true and our reactions to it are the only important issues. This is what Lyotard calls the "unrepresentable" of the postmodern project.

Duras allows her character to break the screen protecting her memories of Nevers, if only to a certain extent, through memory. Various fragments of the "unrepresentable" are given to us. Yet, but for the image of the superimposed hands of the two lovers, the presentation is made through language. The flashbacks in the film cannot be filmic versions of reality. Because they are told to the Japanese man by the French woman, they are creations of her voluntary memory, a fiction, like the reproduction she has seen at the museum and the film in which she has a role. This verbalization of memory has a profound impact on the text and on the reader/spectator. Turim sees it as the catalyst for most of what takes place. "The love affair in the present in *Hiroshima mon amour* is spurred by a desire for narration and transference," she writes (op. cit. 139). Language thus becomes a major actor in the story, replacing visual memory as the principal means of recovering the past, however false the recovered 'text' may be.

The pre-eminence of language in the memory process has gained increased support among theorists. "The concept of 'image memory' has undergone a distinct evolution [. . .]. It is now believed to be mostly a process of encoding and decoding information," writes Turim (ibid. 207). Such encoding and decoding includes, and indeed is dominated by, verbalization. In *Hiroshima* this process has a very specific purpose: remember in order to forget, forget in order to remember. From the first scene, the French woman reveals her need to remember and, thus, the inevitability of forgetting:

> Comme toi, moi aussi j'ai essayé de lutter de toutes mes forces contre l'oubli. Comme toi, j'ai désiré avoir une inconsolable mémoire, une mémoire d'ombres et de pierres. [. . .] J'ai lutté pour mon compte, de toutes mes forces, chaque jour, contre l'horreur de ne plus comprendre du tout le pourquoi de se souvenir. Comme toi, j'ai oublié. Pourquoi nier l'évidente nécessité de la mémoire? (32-33)

The interplay of memory and forgetting is more than an obsession for her; it is her means of carrying on, of regaining control of her "own story" (Borgomano, *L'Écriture filmique* 46).

The French woman does indeed succeed in recapturing what took place in Nevers, and in freeing herself from her love for the German soldier. But the

127

ending that would permit closure is undermined by a variety of forces: desire, subjective memory, lack of distinction between dream and reality, emotional ambivalence resulting from contradictory effects of time on passion, problems of referentiality, and forgetfulness. Memory becomes repetition, "hovering between affirmation and negation, construction and deconstruction, memory and forgetfulness [. . .]. Emphasis is thus on deferral of closure, of memory, of climax and of fixed meaning with a resultant accent on process or production" (Murphy 14). According to Isabelle Raymond, Duras' work is characterized by "la 'circulation' du désir et des personnages" in a fragmented universe "qui demande à s'écrire encore et encore, toujours autrement" (*"Lire le texte . . ."* 82).

The French woman "writes" her story for the first time in fourteen years. In so doing, she feels she has betrayed her German lover and, in the process, lets him slip from memory. But rather than go on to new experiences, she finds herself more embroiled than ever in the indeterminate paths available to her. She is condemned to rewrite continually, always in different contexts—through acting, memory or love affairs—her desire to recapture absolute, impossible love. Desire in Duras' writings becomes a subtext, a series of recurrent narrative palimpsests.

Subversion

Subversion figures among Hassan's postmodern characteristics as that which allows any movement/group/force to break from its predecessor. The constraints of modernism cannot be completely shed, however, so postmodernists employ them in playfulness and parody. For Duras, subversion takes a different form, or more precisely, different forms. Disjunctive elements within the fabric of content and form give a work such as *Hiroshima* its postmodern flavor. The role-playing, exemplified by the French woman performing in a film about Hiroshima (and by the protagonists naming one another "Hiroshima" and "Nevers"), accentuates the postmodern nature of the work. The blurring of dream and reality combined with indeterminacy of theme and form creates a world where nothing and no one is secure.

Memory is a re-writing, a fiction, a subversion of reality. There is the risk of Hiroshima becoming a cliché, a commodity, a betrayal. The transposition of names, for example, from the city to the person, annihilates not only the individual, but the chronology of the narration. This "spatialization of narrative time" (Willis 36)[1] allows Duras the freedom to play with temporality, memory, and desire. Time, space, and form thus become inextricably intertwined in the postmodern scheme.

The final scene of the film reinforces the idea that the individual has been replaced by the universal, informing us of a generalized suffering. The screenplay states it explicitly:

> Elle a réussi à le noyer [le Japonais] dans l'oubli universel.
> Elle en est émerveillée.
>   Elle
> Hi-ro-shi-ma!
>   Elle
> Hi-ro-shi-ma. C'est ton nom!

---

[1] Frederic Jameson also uses the term "the spatialization of time" when describing an aspect of postmodernism: "Time has become a perpetual present and thus spatial. Our relationship to the past is now a spatial one" (Stephanson 6).

Ils se regardent sans se voir. Pour toujours.
   Lui
C'est mon nom. Oui. (On en est là seulement encore.
Et on en restera là pour toujours.) Ton nom à toi est
Nevers. Ne-vers-en-France. (124)

The private story (*histoire*) has been subsumed into
the global context (*Histoire*). The individuals have
forgotten one another and ask us, in turn, to forget
them. All that will remain is whatever reconstruction
of them and of their particular moment in history we
care to make.

Carol Murphy quotes Duras as saying, "A progressive loss of identity is the most desirable experience we can know" (op. cit. 20). The two main
characters of *Hiroshima* have fulfilled this anti-
existentialist desire. The screen memory hides their
factual recollection and precludes us from ever actually seeing or reading their past. Similarly, impossible
love incites the French woman to narrate, to recreate
her past, to remember through forgetting, to forget
through remembering. The progressive loss of identity
comes very close to madness, a subversive loss of reality, "cet anéantissement de velours de sa propre
personne" (*Le Ravissement de Lol V. Stein* 50).

Polychronicity

The shifting perspectives of present and past, the
spatialized present juxtaposed to the narrated memories of the French woman, establish a world with no
fixed chronological limits. We, the reader/spectator,
enjoy a privileged Bergsonian position that allows us
to stand outside the timeline and, in the end, to actually choose which chronological perspective we will
use in trying to understand any given aspect of the

text. This is not simply juggling chronology, but a conscious manipulation of narrative codes that creates alienation in the reader/narrator while affording us freedom of interpretation. Epistemological issues have given way to ontological questions, as the determination of the characters' place in a given world is displaced by the impossible identification of that world.

Roland Barthes' five narrative codes are juggled in *Hiroshima* in a dizzying display of dexterity that leaves us disoriented at the end.[2] The symbolic code, the textual play of power and desire, inevitably dominates the others. This is the scene of the conflict between past and present, the locus of nostalgia where the past becomes an object of desire. The symbolic code maintains the indeterminacy of the text as the French woman struggles to gain control of it through memory. It is thus the ultimate subversion of the traditional totalizing role of memory, which here becomes a source of alienation and repression. It is, like the text itself, a screen memory hiding what has been repressed: the unspeakable.

---

2 In *S/Z* Barthes distinguishes the *proairetic* (real world linear sequence) from the *hermeneutic* (code of enigmas) in which the answer to the question asked is delayed. In the film of *Hiroshima*, flashbacks both resolve and heighten the enigma of the story being recounted. The *semic* code (association of a character with certain connotations) is the psychoanalytic dimension of the characters' personality. As such, it dances in and out of our consciousness, ever-present in the unfolding of the ontological questions posed by the text. The *referential* (historical and scientific knowledge of the culture within fiction) plays a straightforward role in the establishment of the historical context in which "Lui" and "Elle" live and remember. All of these codes are governed in Duras' fiction by the final one, the *symbolic* (textual play of power and desire). For further analysis, see Turim 11.

Films establish a relationship between the spectator and the symbolic code that other genres cannot. "The flashback has become a means for the sound cinema to avoid the static aspects of long verbal renderings and to develop complex narrational modes that combine image and the spoken words," writes Turim (op. cit. 49). The viewer of a film like *Hiroshima mon amour* is forced to become more active, and therefore more involved, in the recreation of the text that takes place every time the film is shown. Each one of us brings to the viewing personal memories and expectations based on what we know of Duras and especially of the experience evoked by her title. We all have an image of what happened at Hiroshima, an image formed for many of us by news footage. The film thus includes the spectator in the contrasting and blending of reality and fiction.

Just one example from the film makes evident the complexity of the symbolic code. When the French woman remembers her German lover's death and the film flashes back to Nevers, the Japanese man "becomes" the German:

    Lui
Quand tu es dans la cave, je suis mort?
    Elle
Tu es mort [. . .] et [. . .]
(Nevers: l'Allemand agonise très lentement sur le quai.)
    Elle
[. . .] comment supporter une telle douleur?

Later in the same scene:

    Lui
Tu cries?
    Elle
Au début, non, je ne crie pas. Je t'appelle doucement.

Lui
Mais je suis mort.
Elle
Je t'appelle quand même. Même mort. Puis un jour, tout
à coup, je crie, je crie très fort comme une sourde. C'est
alors qu'on me met dans la cave pour me punir.
Lui
Tu cries quoi?
Elle
Ton nom allemand. Seulement ton nom. Je n'ai plus
qu'une seule mémoire, celle de ton nom. (90)

This, of course, is precisely how the film will end:
all points of contact are obliterated save the names of
the cities. Here, however, the Japanese, as substitute
for the German, does more than fulfill his role as catalyst for memory. He takes on an identity that troubles the reader/spectator, for it creates a mélange of
memories, both intertextual and historical. Present
becomes past, one lover becomes another, Japanese
becomes German. As the French woman attempts to
recapture what she has repressed, we are more conscious than ever of the complexity of memory and of
its inherently unspeakable nature.

Polychronicity adds to the postmodern nature of
Hiroshima mon amour by throwing the spectator off
track. As expectation is continually thwarted by the
'stop-go' nature of the frames, by the merging of the
various levels of narration, and by the spatialization
of fictive time, avenues of interpretation open in such
an array that no two viewers could come to a single
conclusion. The experience of the French woman and
her two lovers exists only in the interplay of fiction,
historical context, and the present perspective of the
audience. Indeterminacy is then inevitable, since even
individual interpretation and reaction are subject to
deferral of closure and pervasive desire.

Silence and Repetition

One of the advantages that cinema has over the written text is its ability to convey sounds. In *Hiroshima* there are three kinds of sound: dialogue, music, and silence. The three, though disparate and dissonant, work together to form a postmodern silence that simultaneously says everything and nothing.

In the opening scene of the film, we are immediately struck by the music: a repeated, haunting tune whose harsh rhythm plays off the fragmented harmony of the bodies making love. The music announces that this will not be an easy film to watch, that sense will come of it only through the totality of the elements presented, including the music itself. The repetition of the rhythm and tune is quickly familiar to the viewer and even becomes a comforting factor in the first scene. In the body of the film, however, the music does not play the traditional role of setting a background mood. On the contrary, it appears unexpectedly, at times jarring us, reminding us of its presence. At other moments, when we might expect to hear it, it denies us the pleasure. This use of music alienates us not just from the traditional expectations of the role of music in a film, but from the role of music in this particular film. Haunting as it may be, it carries no theme that we can grasp reassuringly. It becomes, instead, part of the network of sounds that make up the language of postmodern silence.

The dialogue parallels the repetitious nature of the music, the rhythm of the utterances of one character echoing that of the other. Each echo, however, contains on a semantic level a change that makes the response the possession of the speaker. As "Elle" contradicts "Lui," the dialogue takes on a difficult harmony, a contrapuntal quality reminiscent of both the music and of the opening love scene:

> Lui
> Tu n'as rien vu à Hiroshima. Rien.
> Elle
> J'ai tout vu. Tout.

Later in the opening scene:

> Elle
> Je n'ai rien inventé.
> Lui
> Tu as tout inventé. (28)

Even when the French woman remembers Nevers, "Lui" questions and prods "Elle" by repeating the terms just used by "her." At the end, when the Japanese lover 'becomes' the German and when "Lui" and "Elle" 'become' the names of their cities, the repetition takes on an almost ghostly quality, as if the words themselves were replacing the disappearing characters:

> Elle
> Hi-ro-shi-ma.
> Elle
> Hi-ro-shi-ma. C'est ton nom.
> Lui
> C'est mon nom, oui. Ton nom à toi est Nevers. Nevers
> en France. (124)

Words lose their semantic value as they are displaced by their break-up into sound patterns that create a dreamlike atmosphere, further blurring distinctions between sensory and "factual" reality. The French woman is remembering as much with her body and her heart as with her mind.

All three levels of narration—story, memory, and history—are punctuated by silences that carry meaning. The lovers' dialogue contains blanks in which desire is palpable. Silence is what Duras calls "un mot-absence, un mot-trou," the creation of a space in which a search for the missing word, the missing moment takes place. Lol V. Stein remains silent because she lacks a word:

> Ç'aurait été un mot-absence, un mot-trou creusé en son centre d'un trou, de ce trou où tous les autres mots auraient été enterrés. On n'aurait pas pu le dire mais on aurait pu le faire résonner [. . .]. Ce mot qui n'existe pas pourtant est là: il vous attend au tournant du langage, il vous défie, il n'a jamais servi, de le soulever, de le faire surgir [. . .]. (48-49)

The lovers of *Hiroshima mon amour* have behind them the fourteen years of silence the French woman has lived since the war. Her narration of the memories of Nevers may be seen as an attempt to fill that silence, but her words are driven by her desire to forget, which prompts the ultimate silence of the "mot-absence," the "mot-trou."

Paralleling the woman's silence are the silent cries of the victims of Hiroshima filmed in the documentaries viewed at the museum. We see in their faces the coming together of memory (expressed in sound and words) and forgetting, the need to relegate the horror of history to the silence of the forgotten.

There are postmodern aspects of *Hiroshima mon amour* that the present essay does not explore. The most evident of these is self-reflexivity: the film's constant reminder that we are watching a movie. The French woman is an actress in a film which is a fiction about an event descriptions of which must be recreations. In costume, she suffers a further loss of identity. We watch the cameras as they become part of the scene in the street demonstration. We see the documentaries which remind us that all films are fiction. Finally, the flashbacks are a visual guide to the form being presented. Only a film can keep us so visibly aware of the experiences it both evokes and unmakes.

Other characteristics of postmodernism are absent from *Hiroshima*, notably playfulness. Duras is not attempting to circumvent modernist/realist tradition through any sort of ludic displacement, such as parody or pastiche. Her concerns incorporate and then transcend questions of form and language. Love, war, and memory combine to create an image of the world as bleak as Beckett's, but without his humor. She has managed to incorporate postwar existential *Angst* into an anti-existential thrust toward loss of self. The experimentation with form parallels, in Duras, her characters' search (most often through memory) for an elusive wholeness.

If postmodernism describes worlds that might be rather than worlds that are, memory assumes a different role. No longer can author, reader, and spectator rely on memory (whether voluntary or involuntary) to provide answers to epistemological questions. In the postmodern world there are only questions, and ontological investigation, in which memory can clearly play a part, opens up an infinite number of possible paths to travel. In the postmodern world, memory is allied with forgetting, structure with fragmentation, construction with subversion, language with silence. While modernists sought "a relationship between narration and the unconscious on one hand and the ludic play of structure on the other," they did so in the identifiable wholeness of a familiar world of language and memory. Postmodernism removes the safety net and sends us tumbling through the air with nowhere to land.

While the field of postmodernism is as undefined as the absence of conclusion inherent in it, valuable questions are raised by a work like *Hiroshima mon amour* about love, war, history, memory, language, film, and the modern world. Questions which, having no answers, provoke us as readers/spectators, through ontological disruption, to create possible worlds of our own.

VIII

IMAGINATION INTO MYTH:
LOVE (LANGUAGE) AS MADNESS
IN PLATO AND DURAS

Inger Gilbert

In the short prose piece titled "Imagination dead, imagine" Samuel Beckett describes both the paralysis and the impossibility of a world without imagination. This paradox is of course inscribed in the title itself which barely finishes uttering its death sentence before rising from its ashes with the imperative, "imagine." The Beckettian tension seems to describe accurately the Durassian enterprise in which narrative also appears to be anchored in a world devoid of movement and spontaneity, of possibility and departure, and yet is flooded with the imperative of desire.

This world disguises a profound malaise, a paralysis of mind, which imagination overwhelms with an irresistible impetuosity and destructive effect reminiscent of the China Sea which used to flood the lands of Mme Donnadieu during Marguerite Duras' childhood in Indochina, making all barricades vain. The Durassian world is a world of "Imagination dead" into which—without warning—the imperative "imagine" intrudes as a destructive force. The Durassian protagonist lives in a world which, at its own peril, has ignored the unforeseen, the irrational, the Dionysian element of its making. That such ignorance is perilous indeed is the Durassian proposal.

In many of Duras' novels erotic love acts as both subject and undoing of subject. The fierceness of this love and its claims cannot be understood or explicated within a Christian, Romantic, or Freudian discourse, but Plato's theories on love as exposed in his *Phaedrus* may serve. Written after *The Republic* and *Symposium*, *Phaedrus* follows the familiar form of the dialogues. The subject is love, but whereas we might have expected some definition according to the utilitarian principles that inform *The Republic*, Socrates here identifies love as madness, divinely inspired. The dialogue takes place on a riverbank outside the city, close to where Boreas, the Northwind, is said to have raped Oreithyia. But legend is not Socrates' concern, and he rejects his friend's questions on the subject, leaving others to anthropomorphize the natural world.

Symposium had laid the groundwork for Plato's thoughts on love (arguing that love is always love *of*, and seeks possession as its goal); *Phaedrus* defines that love as divine madness—"not a thing sent from heaven for the advantage both of lover and beloved [. . .] but as a gift of the gods, fraught with the highest bliss" (58).[1] I am writing this without any knowledge of Greek and so must trust the translator to have chosen the word "fraught" as most accurately describing the meaning of the Greek original. And if "love is madness," then it is perhaps fitting that the con-

---

[1] It is interesting to remember here that Duras' *Agatha* takes on the name of "Diotima" from Plato's *Symposium*. The Platonic connection in Duras may run deeper than hitherto discussed by critics. Editor's note.

notations of "fraught" are negative (as in "a life fraught with unhappiness"), or at least suggest suspense and uncertainty (as in "a trip fraught with danger"). Love, for Plato (as for Duras) is not an "advantage," but "a gift of the gods." The bliss it brings is "fraught."

In a 1975 interview with Susan Husserl-Kapit, Marguerite Duras said that writing is translation, thus implying an original text, a proto-text that is irretrievable, except through the spoken word—a text that is other and doomed to lose its otherness through the powerful grid of self. Thus, writing as translation resembles a birthing, but not necessarily a birth that leads to life. It is perhaps not too farfetched to suggest that the Durassian text, a translation of the wordless, also comes to us fraught with danger and uncertainty. For Duras, words are clearly more important than syntax;[2] their meaning must be fabricated by association, by clustering, by the evocation of anterior connotations and relationships from other contexts. Meaning in Duras will not build up sequentially by accumulation from sentences and paragraphs leading to development, building towards climax and resolution, understanding, appeasement. Even in her private life she refuses "peace" as she responds to a message from Robert Antelme, her former husband, who wanted her to be "apaisée": "Quelle histoire, lui il voudrait me voir tout le temps apaisée, ça dure depuis trente ans" (Andréa 82). Socrates' philosophy and his manner of inquiry also progressed by way of examining individual words and their habitual connotations in order to arrive at new defi-

---

2 See "Premier Entretien" in *Les Parleuses* 11.

141

nitions or questions about previous assumptions. The difference is, of course, that Socrates as a philosopher believed that answers did, ultimately, exist, while Duras as a writer, working through the modes of fiction (opposed not only to reality, but also to the truth which Socrates sought to find), allows no definitions or answers.[3]

As Plato compares the madness of love to the necessary madness of prophets and oracles at holy shrines ("when sane they did little or nothing," *Phaedrus* 56) and the poet's "madness of the Muses," it is interesting to note the close relationship there is in his mind between love—erotic passion—and rhetoric or language. Poetry, oracles, and love: according to Socrates there is an intimate connection between these because they at once stretch but also crucially depend on language for expression. For Socrates, poetry and prophecy represent a mapping of the deepest layers of human consciousness, the same kind of intimate and necessary relationship he postulated for love.[4]

But if language is one of the deepest lodestars of human identity, the passion of love takes us to our very origin of unfallen being. Erotic passion, according to Plato, is inspired by the soul's sojourn among the perfect forms before it fell to Earth and had to live

---

[3] Could we not say, perhaps, that in place of Socrates' nostalgia for a perfection known but lost, Duras offers the melancholia of the unknowable (love, perfection) without accommodation in any time or space? Editor's note.

[4] Of course, such an emphasis on language as both measure and prison-house of human identity also makes Socrates a forerunner of modernist and postmodernist critical concerns, pointing the way toward such diverse "disciples" as Heidegger, Wittgenstein, Kristeva, and Derrida.

in constant search and recollection of former perfection. Thus, when we come across beauty here on
Earth, we are reminded of what we once—in a higher
state—beheld face to face. It is because passion is a
recollection of the divine that it cannot, must not, be
resisted. While Phaedrus understands this argument,
we may wonder at Socrates' abdication of rational
discourse in defense of madness, but then Plato was
no novelist, and about the problems of negotiating the
expression of this madness in narrative language, he
remains silent.

In his search for self-knowledge and morality,
Socrates wanted to show that even in erotic love, the
most selfish of all human pursuits, we still act under
profound moral injunction, because we are impelled
to fulfill our destiny as lovers of beauty and perfection. This love has nothing to do with friendship
or family relationships: "He is filled with amazement,
for he perceives that all his other friends and kinsmen
have nothing to offer in comparison with this friend
in whom there dwells a god" (*Phaedrus* 105), because
ultimately love represents love of our own selves,
"your lover is as it were a mirror in which you behold
yourself" (ibid. 106). In Duras, most couples and
other family relationships ultimately fail for the same
reason. For her, as for Plato, love is a mirror-image,
the salvaging of a contract with our own selves, an
establishment of our truest identity. In passion we
betray our own origin in that same beauty and perfection we are pursuing. Thus for Plato and Duras,
ultimately it is imaginative life as opposed to rational
argument or social convention that defines the deepest
needs, the highest aspirations of human identity.
With the collapse of rational argument so eloquently

and painfully described in the Beckettian canon, our options seem narrower than Plato's.

We fall in love, Plato says, because we remember. In deconstructionist terms, subconsciously we are "always already" in love and so, when such "always already" lovers meet, the force of their mutual attraction is felt as both a powerful interruption and a long-awaited fulfillment of their lives. Love causes the soul to regrow the wings it had lost upon falling to Earth, Plato said, and given his argument so firmly anchored in a mythology which both wounds and heals, readers of *Phaedrus* have yielded to its persuasion, as we have—in our language, in our actions, in our fictions, both narrative and other. We may no longer believe in souls with wings or Eternal Forms (and it is doubtful that Socrates himself, that paragon of rationality, saw such images as other than heuristic devices expressing a reality that lived in language alone); yet, culturally, love as destiny remains a powerful fiction.

It is everywhere apparent that the myth of erotic passion has acquired overlays of Christian as well as Freudian and Romantic discourses that dilute the Socratic fatality with notions of biology, choice, sexuality, gender, sin and chastity, family and progeny. The kind of erotic passion apparent between, say, a Heathcliff and a Catherine, where each of the protagonists literally would become the other ("I am Heathcliff," in Cathy's famous exclamation), is the exception, and that love finds poor accommodation in a culture such as ours, circumscribed as it is by notions of self-determination and autonomy.

But the Platonic heritage of love as madness has survived the tightly packed narrative of the nineteenth century to re-emerge in the sparser, less securely anchored world of postmodernism. Instead of authority, the writer now has only language to fill up the interior spaces between characters, to describe their comings and goings. In a sense, the Platonic dialogue has been restored to its initial economy with its emphasis on language as the sole vehicle of action. With an important difference, however. Whereas Plato used language linearly to amass his arguments and persuade by reason and logic, narrative fiction, since its abandonment of chronology and accumulation, now must endeavor to bend language into image and possibility. Instead of extrinsically trying to persuade, language now must seek illumination from within. In so doing, it becomes recursive, hypothetical, provisional, repetitive, as it looks to define and discover the lives of its speakers, and the geographies they inhabit. Plato divided *Phaedrus* into two sections—one dealing with erotic passion, and the other with the art of verbal persuasion. In fictional narrative which moves from talking about to being (passion), language is challenged into becoming the main protagonist of the text.

Love/passion in Duras is characterized by two factors: the physical beauty of the beloved and the inevitability of the passion this beauty will inspire: "love as madness"—love which cannot be humanized (that is, coded into language and reason) because it has its origin in a world transcending human language and rationale. It was Plato's struggle to construct an argument about that which in another world existed in rapt contemplation, word-less because beyond the need for words. It was Duras' to invent the fictional language describing such a world.

Erotic passion in Duras is always calamitous and cannot find accommodation within the quotidian. In her universe, language, in endeavoring to mirror the

145

madness it reflects, falters, fails, breaks down, cannot move to syntax, to proposition, to argument. As the Durassian text struggles to voice feelings and needs which originate in wordlessness—not because of a lack, but because of a fullness of meaning, because of a meaning that refuses abbreviation into words—readers are left with a fiction without boundaries, a story without names or endings. A fiction which is ultimately about the condition of fiction itself. And from condition of fiction to human condition the text is obviously only a reader away.

The film and the screenplay of *Hiroshima mon amour* come to mind here as powerfully illustrative. Even though writing is translation (according to Duras), "Hiroshima" and "mon amour" are untranslatable and thus rely on readers/viewers to interpret according to their own resources the two French words and the name of the Japanese city. The three words operate within an oxymoronic relationship, in that the placename with its historical reference to death and destruction yet is followed by an intimate term of endearment. But how can anyone say "mon amour" to "Hiroshima," and what can "Hiroshima" mean to "mon amour"?[5] The film/script itself occurs within this tension, and though it deals with a historical event, it does so from two different perspectives: one Eastern, one Western, one male, one female. Ul-

---

[5] Deborah Glassman comments, "*Hiroshima* is proclaimed as a technically innovative and insightful film. The title, however, which is a program for reading the film, has been too little commented upon. We can parse it as Hiroshima *et* mon amour, Hiroshima *est* mon amour, Hiroshima *ou* mon amour or Hiroshima, mon amour! What is the link? Hiroshima is an overdetermined proper noun [. . .]" (*Fascinating Vision . . .* 26). Editor's note.

timately, the film transcends its own historicity and form and becomes an illustration less solved than posited of a possible relationship between fiction and life, past and present, loss and redemption, death and life.

Duras' *Emily L.* also illustrates this double relationship between fiction and life. For the first- and second-person pronouns employed in the novel it is tempting to substitute names that would indicate autobiographical relations, if only for the references to a childhood spent in the Orient and the preoccupation with writing (both obviously attributable to Duras herself). But if "I" and "you" are supposed to represent some sort of reality, it is a reality that feeds and crucially depends on the fictional couple disguised under their third-person pronouns. That is to say that Duras (and her companion) may be physically present in the text which thus accurately describes a certain summer and a certain preoccupation in the life of Duras. Yet it is to the extent that the fictional can be injected into reality that the latter becomes revitalized and can find a way out of its own impasse. In her obvious pain caused by a changing relationship, Duras, the person, can then ask via the text, "Is this what you and I would have wanted?" and perhaps find meaning and understanding in her writing, imagining, of *Emily L.* While the narrative "I" and "you" may be suffering a crisis in their relationship, it is clear that Emily L. and the Captain have been united by love as "madness" over a lifetime. It is also obvious that this "madness" excluded any other occupation. When the baby dies, there are no more children. When Emily L.'s poems acquire literary fame, she has long since stopped writing. She and the Captain who "ne la quitte pas des yeux, jamais" (97) spend a life-

147

time on their yacht, sailing on the seven seas: "Si seuls au monde ils étaient, ils ne savaient plus rien de la solitude" (91).

While Emily L.'s parents opposed the marriage, they, like all their counterparts in the Durassian fiction, also knew not to prevent the lovers' relationship. This cooperation between lovers and the outside world points to another similarity between the texts of Plato and Duras. Simultaneously with the depiction of the "madness of love," there is in *Emily L.* a curious display of rationality, of good manners, of courtesy and intelligence orchestrating and bathing the novel's darkness, its frenzied passion, in a kind of *lucidité*. It is clear that the protagonists, caught up in a relentless pursuit of beauty and passion, as well as their counterparts (those they either betray or bypass) acknowledge the power and the priority of love. Along with ecstasy, there is pain and anguish in a Durassian novel. But what we rarely encounter in her mature work is jealousy, vindictiveness, anger. In a true Platonic hierarchy of expression, such "inferior" feelings cannot coexist with the "higher" feelings of love and passion. "Jealousy has no place in the choir divine," said Socrates (*Phaedrus* 70).

But love itself is a jealous god and will suffer no rival preoccupations. Emily L. gave up her poetry because she felt it "comme un terrible défaut aussi qu'elle aurait attrapé au-dehors de sa vie" (121). When the narrator-couple meets them, "c'était impossible de franchir le silence qui les séparait des autres gens" (128). It is on the last page that the narrator understands that only writing can match or mirror their life. Writing gets through to "le corps qui lit et qui veut connaître l'histoire depuis les origines, et à chaque lecture ignorer toujours plus avant que ce qu'il ignore déjà" (153). Writing not as proposition and conclusion, but as a "mise-en-abyme," a circular spin, a maelstrom, that must follow its own momentum in Duras' well-known *écriture courante*. Like love, it must not be manipulated, controlled, corrected. Instead, the writer must leave "l'écriture entière avec le reste, ne rien assagir, ni vitesse, ni lenteur, laisser tout dans l'état de l'apparition" (154).

This is the last sentence of *Emily L.*, but its theme was introduced earlier in statements like, "Je ne sais pas si l'amour est un sentiment. Parfois je crois qu'aimer c'est voir. C'est vous voir" (139). In the relationship between love and language both must constantly re-invent each other in order to cast a probe that is deep enough. Socrates says in *Phaedrus* that "sight is the keenest mode of perception vouchsafed us through the body" (93). If writing has shown the Durassian narrator that the body must be the lens through which true narrative comes into being, we can perhaps rewrite the "madness" of love as the "authenticity" of love. When writing is grounded in the body, we are finally awakened from our long-poisoned sleep, begun when we stung ourselves on the Cartesian spindle of the separation (and the hierarchization) of body and mind. Wakened by a kiss, so to speak. To see. Again. For eyes unused to light such seeing can be blinding.

For Emily L. and the Captain, the stories and the letter remain "plus fort que la mort." For them, the problem "qui avait dû se poser devait être celui du temps qu'il y avait à vivre. Cela sans en enlever un seul jour, une seule heure, un seul lieu, une seule phrase" (95). The problem, and also the felicity, but not necessarily a felicity that language or living can convey.

SELECTIVE BIBLIOGRAPHY

Listed here are only those primary and secondary sources actually referenced in the preceding essays. For a more detailed bibliography, see Ricouart, given below.

Ames, Sanford S. *Remains to be seen. Essays on Marguerite Duras.* New York: Peter Lang, 1988.

Andréa, Yann. *M.D.* Paris: Minuit, 1983.

Armel, Aliette. *Marguerite Duras et l'autobiographie.* Paris: Le Castor Astral, 1990.

Assouline, Pierre. "Mes amours, c'est moi." *Lire* 193, October 1991.

Bachelard, Gaston. *L'Air et les songes; Essai sur l'imagination du mouvement.* Paris: José Corti, 1943.

Bajomée, Danielle, and Ralph Heyndels. *Ecrire dit-elle: imaginaires de Marguerite Duras.* Bruxelles: Editions de l'Université de Bruxelles, 1985.

Beauvoir, Simone de. *The Second Sex.* Trans. & ed. H. M. Parshley. New York: Vintage, 1952.

Borgomano, Madeleine. *Duras: Une lecture des fantasmes.* Petit Roeulx, Belgium: CISTRE, 1985.

———. *L'Ecriture filmique de Marguerite Duras.* Paris: Albatros, 1985.

Bremondy, Gisèle: "La Destruction de la réalité." *L'Arc* 98, 1985.

Camus, Renaud. *Notes achriennes.* Paris: P.O.L., 1984.

150

Carré, Jean-Marie, ed. *Lettres de la vie littéraire d'Arthur Rimbaud*. Paris: Gallimard, 1990.

Cixous, Hélène. "Fiction and Its Phantoms: A Reading of Freud's 'Das Unheimliche'." *New Literary History* 7, 1976. Originally published as "La fiction et ses fantômes," *Poétique* 10, 1972.

――――. *Jours de l'an*. Paris: Des Femmes, 1990.

Clément, Catherine. *The Newly Born Woman*. Trans. Betsy Wing. Minneapolis: U of Minnesota P, 1986.

Cohen, Susan. "Phantasm and Narration in Marguerite Duras' *The Ravishing of Lol V. Stein*." In *The Psychoanalytic Study of Literature*. Eds. Joseph Reppen and Maurice Charney. Hillsdale, NJ: The Analytic P, 1985.

Derrida, Jacques. "Plato's Pharmacy." In *Dissemination*. Urbana & Chicago: U of Chicago P, 1981.

DiBattista, Maria. "The Clandestine Fictions of Marguerite Duras." In *Breaking the Sequence: Women's Experimental Fiction*. Eds. Ellen G. Friedman and Ellen Fuchs. Princeton, NJ: Princeton UP, 1989.

Doubrovsky, Serge. *Autobiographiques: de Corneille à Sartre*. Paris: P.U.F., 1988.

Druon, Michèle. "La 'maladie de la mort' du sujet dans *India Song*: Une allégorie postmoderne." *L'Esprit créateur* 30, Spring 1990.

Duraille, Marguerite. *Virginie Q* . Roman présenté par Patrick Rambaud. Paris: Balland, 1988.

Duras, Marguerite. *Un Barrage contre le Pacifique*. Paris: Gallimard, 1950.

――――. *Le Marin de Gibraltar*. Paris: Gallimard, 1952.

151

———. *Moderato cantabile*. Paris: Minuit, 1958.

———. *Dix heures et demie du soir en été*. Paris: Gallimard, 1960.

———. *Hiroshima mon amour*. Paris: Gallimard, 1960.

———. *Le Ravissement de Lol V. Stein*. Paris: Gallimard, 1964.

———. *Le Vice-consul*. Paris: Gallimard, 1965.

———. *Détruire dit-elle*. Paris: Minuit, 1969.

———. *India Song*. Films Armorial, 1975.

———. *Le Camion, suivi de Entretien avec Michelle Porte*. Paris: Minuit, 1977.

———. *L'Eté 80*. Paris: Minuit, 1980.

———. *L'Homme atlantique*. Paris: Minuit, 1982.

———. *La Maladie de la mort*. Paris: Minuit, 1982.

———. *L'Amant*. Paris: Minuit, 1984.

———. *Les Yeux bleus cheveux noirs*. Paris: Minuit, 1986.

———. *La Pute de la côte normande*. Paris: Minuit, 1986.

———. *La Vie matérielle*. Paris: P.O.L., 1987.

———. *L'Amante anglaise*. Paris: Gallimard, 1987.

———. *Emily L*. Paris: Minuit, 1987.

———. *La Pluie d'été*. Paris: P.O.L., 1990.

———. *L'Amant de la Chine du Nord*. Paris: Gallimard, 1991.

———. *Le Monde extérieur.* Paris: P.O.L., 1992.

——— and Xavière Gauthier. *Les Parleuses.* Paris: Minuit, 1974.

——— and Michelle Porte. *Les Lieux de Marguerite Duras.* Paris: Minuit, 1977.

———. *Marguerite Duras à Montréal.* Texte réunis et présentés par Suzanne Lamy et André Roy. Paris: Spirale et Solin, 1984.

——— and Bernard Pivot. "Apostrophes." Antenne 2, September 1984.

Eagleton, Terry. *Literary Theory: An Introduction.* Minneapolis: U of Minnesota P, 1983.

Ehrenzweig, Anton. *The Hidden Order of Art.* Berkeley, CA: U of California P, 1967.

Elliot, Robert C. *The Literary Persona.* Urbana & Chicago: U of Chicago P, 1982.

Etienne, Marie-France. "L'Oubli et la répétition: *Hiroshima mon amour.*" *Romanic Review* 78:4, 1987.

Evans, Martha Noel. *Masks of Tradition: Women and the Politics of Writing in Twentieth-Century France.* Ithaca & London: Cornell UP, 1987.

Felman, Shoshana. *Jacques Lacan and the Adventure of Insight: Psychoanalysis in Contemporary Culture.* Cambridge & London: Harvard UP, 1987.

Freud, Sigmund. *Beyond the Pleasure Principle* Trans. James Strachey. New York: W.W. Norton, 1961.

———. "Mourning and Melancholia." *The Standard Edition of the Complete Psychological Works of Sigmund Freud*, vol. 14. Ed. J. Strachey. London: Hogarth, 1951.

———. "The Uncanny." In *Collected Papers* XVII. London: Hogarth, 1950. Originally published as "Das Unheimliche," *Imago* 5, 1919.

Genette, Gérard. *Palimpsestes* Paris: Seuil, 1982.

———. *Seuils.* Paris: Seuil, 1987.

Glassman, Deborah N. *Marguerite Duras. Fascinating Vision and Narrative Cure.* London & Toronto: Associated UP, 1991.

Grosz, Elizabeth. *Jacques Lacan: A feminist introduction.* London & New York: Routledge, 1990.

———. *Sexual Subversions: Three French Feminists.* Sydney: Allen & Unwin, 1989.

Guers-Villate, Yvonne. *Continuité/discontinuité de l'œuvre durassienne.* Brussels: Editions de l'Université de Bruxelles, 1985.

Hassan, Ihab. *The Postmodern Turn.* Columbus, OH: Ohio State UP, 1987.

Hewitt, Leah D. *Autobiographical Tightropes: Simone de Beauvoir, Nathalie Sarraute, Marguerite Duras, Monique Wittig, and Maryse Condé.* Lincoln, NE: U of Nebraska P, 1990.

Higgins, Dick. *A Dialectic of Centuries: Notes Towards a Theory of the New Arts.* New York: Printed Editions, 1978.

Hofmann, Carol. *Forgetting and Marguerite Duras.* Niwot, CO: U of Colorado P, 1991.

Husserl-Kapit, Susan. "An Interview with Marguerite Duras." *Signs* 1, 1975.

Irigaray, Luce. *Speculum of the other woman.* Trans. Gillian C. Gill. Ithaca & London: Cornell UP, 1985.

Kristeva, Julia. *Black Sun: Depression and Melancholia.* Trans. Léon S. Roudiez. New York: Columbia UP, 1989.

———. "Héréthique de l'amour." *Tel Quel* 74, Winter 1977.

———. *The Kristeva Reader.* Ed. Toril Moi. New York: Columbia UP, 1986.

———. *Pouvoirs de l'horreur.* Paris: Seuil, 1980.

———. *Tales of Love.* Trans. Léon S. Roudiez. New York: Columbia UP, 1987.

Lacan, Jacques. *Ecrits.* Trans. Alan Sheridan. New York: W.W. Norton, 1977.

———. "Hommage fait à Marguerite Duras, du *Ravissement de Lol V. Stein.*" In *Marguerite Duras.* Paris: Albatros, 1975.

———. *Le Séminaire I: Les Ecrits techniques de Freud.* Paris: Seuil, 1975.

———. *Le Séminaire XX: Encore.* Paris: Seuil, 1975.

———. *Le Séminaire: L'éthique de la psychanalyse.* Paris: Seuil, 1986.

Lejeune, Philippe. *Le Pacte autobiographique.* Paris: Seuil, 1975.

Lydon, Mary. "The Forgetfulness of Memory: Jacques Lacan, Marguerite Duras, and the Text." *Contemporary Literature* xxxix:3, 1988.

Lyotard, Jean-François. *La Condition postmoderne: rapport sur le savoir.* Paris: Minuit, 1979.

———. *The Postmodern Condition: A Report on Knowledge.* Trans. Geoff Bennington and Brian Massumi. Minneapolis: U of Minnesota P, 1984.

Marini, Marcelle. *Territoires du féminin avec Marguerite Duras.* Paris: Minuit, 1977.

McHale, Brian. *Postmodern Fiction.* New York: Methuen, 1987.

Michel, Jacqueline. *Une mise en récit du Silence.* Paris: José Corti, 1986.

Miller, Jacques-Alain, ed. *The Seminar of Jacques Lacan I.* 1957. Trans. John Forrester. Cambridge & New York: Cambridge UP, 1988.

Montrelay, Michèle. *L'Ombre et le Nom.* Paris: Minuit, 1977.

Murphy, Carol. *Alienation and Absence in the Novels of Marguerite Duras.* Nicholasville, KY: French Forum Monographs, 1982.

———. "Duras's *Beast in the Jungle* : Writing Fear (or fear of writing) in *Emily L..*" *Neophilologus* 75, 1991.

Olney, James. *Metaphors of Self: The Meaning of Autobiography.* Princeton, NJ: Princeton UP, 1972.

Papin, Liliane. *L'Autre scène: Le Théâtre de Marguerite Duras.* Saratoga, CA: Anma Libri, 1988.

Pierrot, Jean. *Marguerite Duras.* Paris: José Corti, 1986.

Plato's *Phaedrus.* Trans. R. Hackforth. Cambridge & New York: Cambridge UP, 1987.

Raymond, Isabelle. "Lire le film/voir le texte." *L'Arc* 98, 1985.

Ricouart, Janine. *Ecriture Féminine et Violence. Une Etude de Marguerite Duras.* Birmingham, AL: Summa Publications, 1991.

Robbe-Grillet, Alain. Unpublished interview, New York, 2 October 1991.

Schuster, Jean and Marguerite Duras. "Entretien de Marguerite Duras avec Jean Schuster." In *Marguerite Duras ou le Temps de détruire.* Ed. Alain Vircondelet. Paris: Seghers, 1972.

Selous, Trista. *The Other Woman: Feminism and Femininity in the Work of Marguerite Duras.* New Haven & London: Yale UP, 1988.

156

Shapiro, Stephen. "The Dark Continent of Literature: Autobiography." In *Comparative Literature Studies* 5, 1969.

Spacks, Patricia Meyer. *Imagining a Self: Autobiography and the Novel in Eighteenth Century England.* Cambridge, MA: Harvard UP, 1976.

Spitzer, Leo. "Notes on the Poetic and Empirical 'I' in Medieval Authors." *Tradition* I:4, 1946.

Stamelman, Richard. *Lost Beyond Telling. Representations of Death and Absence in Modern French Poetry.* Ithaca & London: Cornell UP, 1990.

Stephanson, Anders. "Regarding Postmodernism—Conversation with Frederic Jameson." In *Universal Abandon? The Politics of Postmodernism.* Ed. Andrew Ross. Edinburgh: Edinburgh UP, 1988.

Suda, David. *The Moving Image.* Boston, MA: UP of America, 1989.

Suleiman, Susan. "Nadja, Dora, Lol V. Stein: women, madness and narrative." Ed. Shlomith Rimmon-Kenan. In *Discourse in Psychoanalysis and Literature.* London: Methuen, 1987.

Swift, Jonathan. *Journal to Stella.* Ed. Harold Williams. 2vv. Oxford: Clarendon P, 1948.

Turim, Maureen. *Flashbacks in Film: Memory and History.* New York: Routledge, Chapman & Hall, 1989.

Vircondelet, Alain. *Duras.* Paris: François Bourin, 1992.

Willis, Sharon. *Marguerite Duras: Writing on the Body.* Urbana & Chicago: U of Illinois P, 1987.

NOTES ON CONTRIBUTORS

Julia Balén is a graduate associate at the University of Arizona, where she is completing her Ph.D. in comparative literature with a dissertation titled, "Embodied Subjectivities: En/gendering Power in the Construction of Selves."

Julia Lauer-Chéenne is an instructor at the University of Nebraska-Lincoln, where she completed her doctoral dissertation on "Theme and Image in Marguerite Duras," directed by Marshall Olds. She is a contributor to *French Women Writers* (Greenwood Press, 1991) and active in the visual arts.

Rachael Criso is a lecturer in French at the University of Michigan. She received her B.A. in French and German from the University of Sheffield, England, and is a Ph.D. candidate at the University of Pennsylvania, working with Gerald Prince on "Jean Echenoz: Genre Parodist, Literary Ludic and Postmodern Novelist." Her article on "Postmodernism in Contemporary French Literature" is forthcoming in *Romance Languages Annual*, 1992.

Marie-France Etienne is associate professor of French at Hobart and William Smith Colleges. Her dissertation on Gérard de Nerval was directed by Kurt Weinberg at the University of Rochester and published in 1987 by Peter Lang (*Gérard de Nerval: Janus multiplié*). She has written articles on Claudel and Nerval. Her work on Marguerite Duras has appeared in *Romanic Review*, winter 1988.

Inger Gilbert is assistant professor of English and comparative literature at Worcester State College. She began her undergraduate work in Denmark and earned her Ph.D. in comparative literature at the University of Washington with a dissertation on "Narratives of the First Person. Language and Imagination from Rousseau to Beckett," directed by Leroy Searle. She has published on Joyce and Rilke in *Comparative Literature Studies* 26:4, 1989.

Anne-Marie Gronhovd is assistant professor of French at Gustavus Adolphus College, where she also teaches women's studies and Québécois literature. After working on a law degree at the University of Lyon, she completed her dissertation on Marcel Proust at the University of Minnesota. She serves on the editorial board of *The Journal of Durassian Studies* founded by Janine Ricouart.

Robin Lydenberg is professor and director of the Ph.D. program in English at Boston College. Her dissertation in comparative literature dealt with "Lautréamont and the Self-Conscious Novel" (Cornell University). She has written and co-edited books on William Burroughs (U of Illinois P, 1987; Southern Illinois UP, 1991) and published articles on modern fiction in, among others, *Diacritics*, *Contemporary Literature*, and *Modern Fiction Studies*.

Thomas Spear is assistant professor of French at CUNY-Lehman College. His Ph.D. dissertation on "Céline's Autofiction" was directed by Erika Ostrovsky at New York University. He is currently completing a book on autofictive narratives and an anthology of essays on Céline. He has written articles on French and francophone literature for *Yale French Studies*, *Studies in the Novel*, and *French Literature Series*.

William C. VanderWolk is associate professor of French at Bowdoin College. His Ph.D. dissertation on Gustave Flaubert was directed by Stirling Haig at UNC-Chapel Hill. His work on *Hiroshima mon amour* was begun with Anne-Marie Gronhovd in an NEH seminar on postmodernism directed by Ihab Hassan at the University of Wisconsin-Milwaukee, 1989.

𝔖cripta 𝔥umanistica®

Directed by
BRUNO M. DAMIANI
The Catholic University of America
COMPREHENSIVE LIST OF PUBLICATIONS *

1. Everett W. Hesse, The "Comedia" and Points of View. $24.50
2. Marta Ana Diz, Patronio y Lucanor: la lectura inteligente "en el tiempo que es turbio." Prólogo de John Esten Keller. $26.00
3. James F. Jones, Jr., The Story of a Fair Greek of Yesteryear. A Translation from the French of Antoine-François Prévost's L'Histoire d'une Grecque moderne. With Introduction and Selected Bibliography. $30.00
4. Colette H. Winn, Jean de Sponde: Les sonnets de la mort ou La Poétique de l'accoutumance. Préface par Frédéric Deloffre. $22.50
5. Jack Weiner, "En busca de la justicia social: estudio sobre el teatro español del Siglo de Oro." $24.50
6. Paul A. Gaeng, Collapse and Reorganization of the Latin Nominal Flection as Reflected in Epigraphic Sources. Written with the assistance of Jeffrey T. Chamberlin. $24.00
7. Edna Aizenberg, The Aleph Weaver: Biblical, Kabbalistic, and Judaic Elements in Borges. $25.00
8. Michael G. Paulson and Tamara Alvarez-Detrell, Cervantes, Hardy, and "La fuerza de la sangre." $25.50
9. Rouben Charles Cholakian, Deflection/Reflection in the Lyric Poetry of Charles d'Orléans: A Psychosemiotic Reading. $25.00
10. Kent P. Ljungquist, The Grand and the Fair: Poe's Landscape Aesthetics and Pictorial Techniques. $27.50
11. D.W. McPheeters, Estudios humanísticos sobre la "Celestina." $20.00
12. Vittorio Felaco, The Poetry and Selected Prose of Camillo Sbarbaro. Edited and Translated by Vittorio Felaco. With a Preface by Franco Fido. $25.00
13. María del C. Candau de Cevallos, Historia de la lengua española. $33.00
14. Renaissance and Golden Age Studies in Honor of D.W. McPheeters. Ed. Bruno M. Damiani. $30.00
15. Bernardo Antonio González, Parábolas de identidad: Realidad interior y estrategia narrativa en tres novelistas de posguerra. $28.00
16. Carmelo Gariano, La Edad Media (Aproximación Alfonsina). $30.00
17. Gabriella Ibieta, Tradition and Renewal in "La gloria de don Ramiro". $27.50
18. Estudios literarios en honor de Gustavo Correa. Eds. Charles Faulhaber, Richard Kinkade, T.A. Perry. Preface by Manuel Durán. $25.00
19. George Yost, Pieracci and Shelly: An Italian Ur-Cenci. $27.50

20. Zelda Irene Brooks, *The Poetry of Gabriel Celaya*. $26.00
21. *La relación o naufragios de Alvar Núñez Cabeza de Vaca*, eds. Martin A. Favata y José B. Fernández. $27.50
22. Pamela S. Brakhage, *The Theology of "La Lozana andaluza."* $27.50
23. Jorge Checa, *Gracián y la imaginación arquitectónica*. $28.00
24. Gloria Gálvez Lira, *Maria Luisa Bombal: realidad y fantasía*. $28.50
25. Susana Hernández Araico, *Ironía y tragedia en Calderón*. $25.00
26. Philip J. Spartano, *Giacomo Zanella: Poet, Essayist, and Critic of the "Risorgimento."* Preface by Roberto Severino. $24.00
27. E. Kate Stewart, *Arthur Sherburne Hardy: Man of American Letters*. Preface by Louis Budd. $28.50
28. Giovanni Boccaccio, *The Decameron*. English Adaptation by Carmelo Gariano. $30.00
29. Giacomo A. Striuli, "Alienation in Giuseppe Berto". $26.50
30. Barbara Mujica, *Iberian Pastoral Characters*. Preface by Frederick A. de Armas. $33.00
31. Susan Niehoff McCrary, *"'El último godo' and the Dynamics of the Urdrama."* Preface by John E. Keller. $27.50
32. *En torno al hombre y a sus monstruos: ensayos críticos sobre la novelística de Carlos Rojas*, editados por Cecilia Castro Lee y C. Christopher Soufas, Jr. $31.50
33. J. Thomas O'Connell, *Mount Zion Field*. $24.50
34. Francisco Delicado, *Portrait of Lozana: The Lusty Andalusian Woman*. Translation, introduction and notes by Bruno M. Damiani. $45.50
35. Elizabeth Sullam, *Out of Bounds*. Foreword by Michael G. Cooke. $23.50
36. Sergio Corsi, *Il "modus digressivus" nella "Divina Commedia."* $28.75
37. Juan Bautista Avalle-Arce, *Lecturas (Del temprano Renacimiento a Valle Inclán)*. $28.50
38. Rosendo Díaz-Peterson, *Las novelas de Unamuno*. Prólogo de Antonio Carreño. $30.00
39. Jeanne Ambrose, *Syntaxe Comparative Français-Anglais*. $29.50
40. Nancy Marino, *La serranilla española: notas para su historia e interpretación*. $28.75.
41. Carolyn Kreiter-Kurylo, *Contrary Visions*. Preface by Peter Klappert. $24.50
42. Giorgio Perissinotto, *Reconquista y literatura medieval: cuatro ensayos*. $29.50
43. Rick Wilson, *Between a Rock and a Heart Place*. $25.00
44. *Feminine Concerns in Contemporary Spanish Fiction by Women*. Edited by Roberto C. Manteiga, Carolyn Galerstein and Kathleen McNerney. $35.00
45. Pierre L. Ullman, *A Contrapuntal Method For Analyzing Spanish Literature*. $41.50

95. Rosalía Fernández Cabezón, *Cómo leer a Leandro Fernández de Moratín*. $43.50
96. José Angel Ascunce Arrieta, *Cómo leer a Blas de Otero*. $46.50
97. Alicia H. Puleo, *Cómo leer a Julio Cortázar*. $42.50
98. María Eugenia Lacarra Lanz, *Cómo leer "La Celestina"*. $45.50
99. Francisco Garrote Pérez, *Cómo leer el "Lazarillo"*. $43.00
100. Juergen Hahn, *Miracles, Duels, and Cide Hamete's Moorish Dissent*. $42.50
101. Mechthild Cranston, *In Language and in Love—Marguerite Duras: The Unspeakable*. $46.75
102. Gerhard Hauck, *Reductionism in Drama and The Theater: The Case of Samuel Beckett*. $59.50

BOOK ORDERS

* Clothbound. *All book orders*, except library orders, must be prepaid and addressed to **Scripta Humanistica**, 1383 Kersey Lane, Potomac, Maryland 20854. *Manuscripts* to be considered for publication should be sent to the same address.

www.ingramcontent.com/pod-product-compliance
Lightning Source LLC
Chambersburg PA
CBHW020810100426
42814CB00001B/5